THIS BOOK BELONGS TO

CAKE

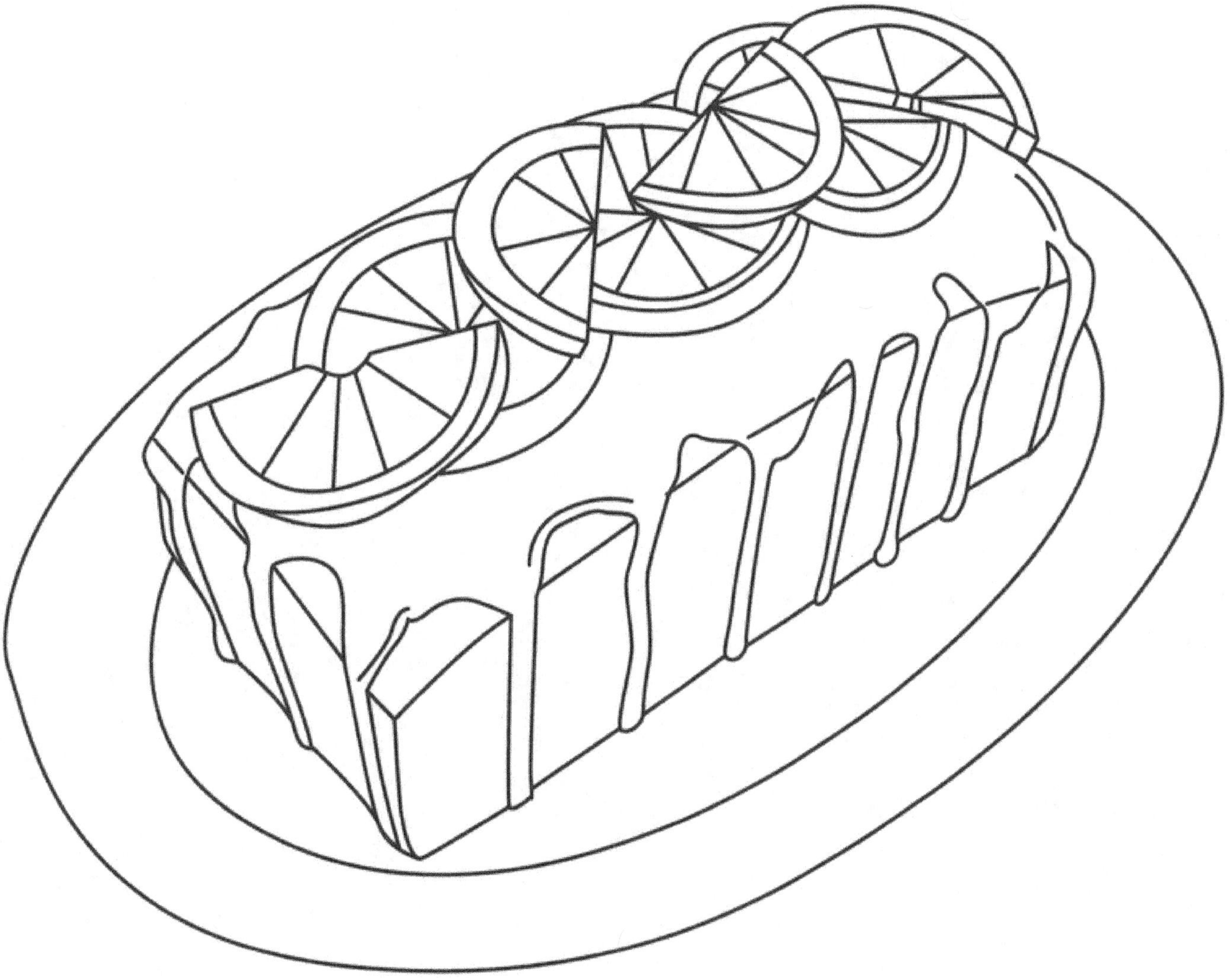

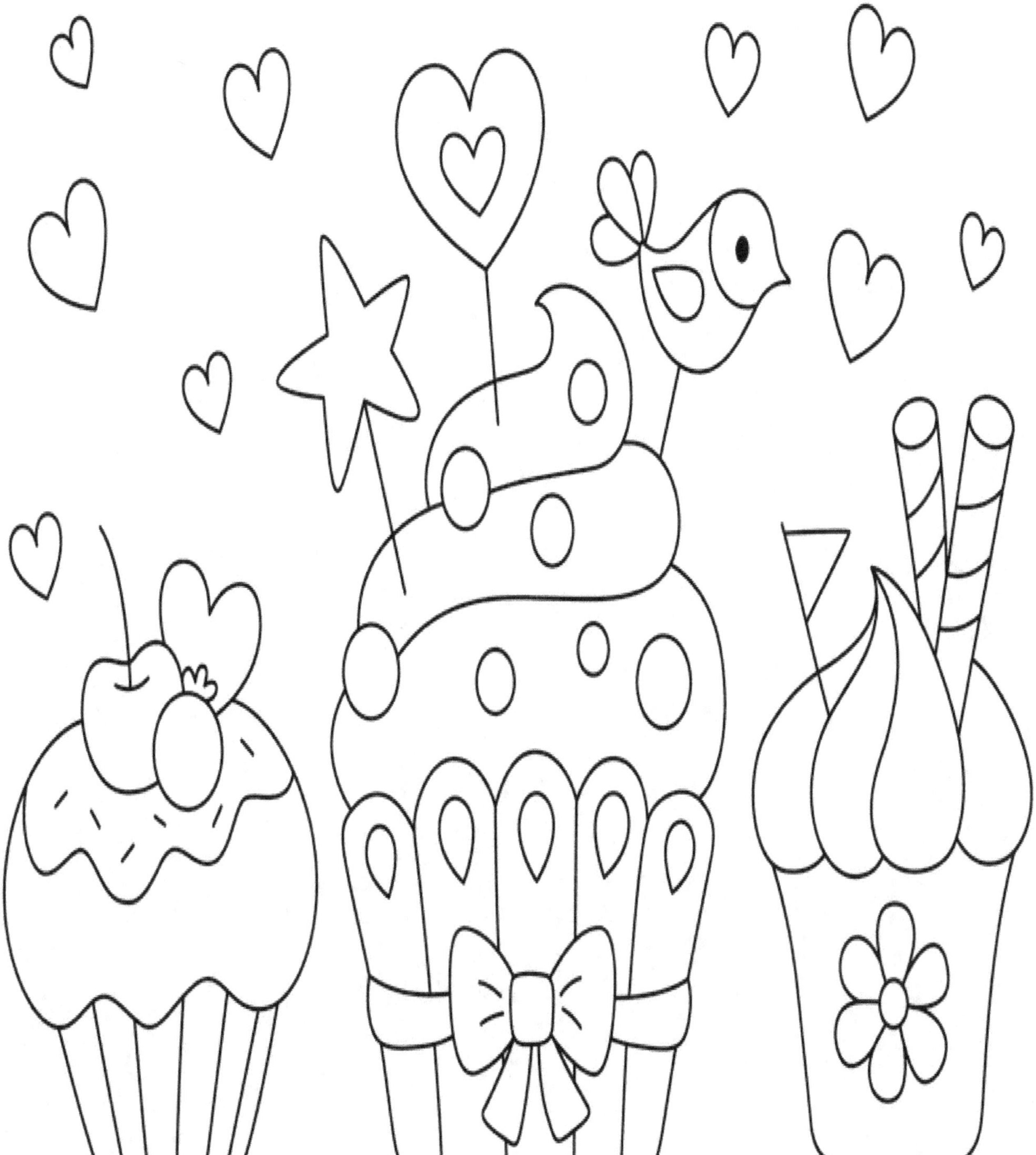

BROWNIE

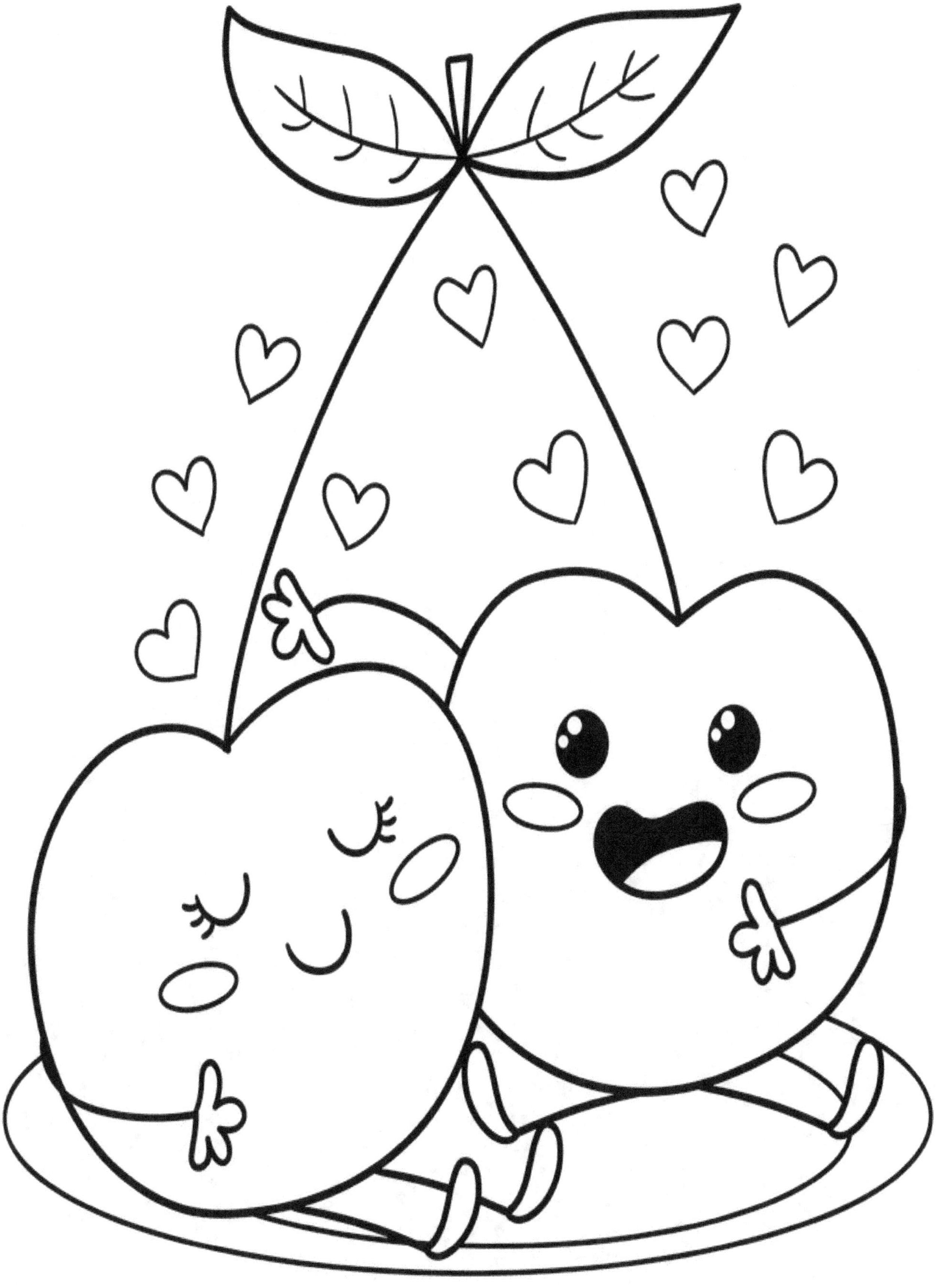

CAKE

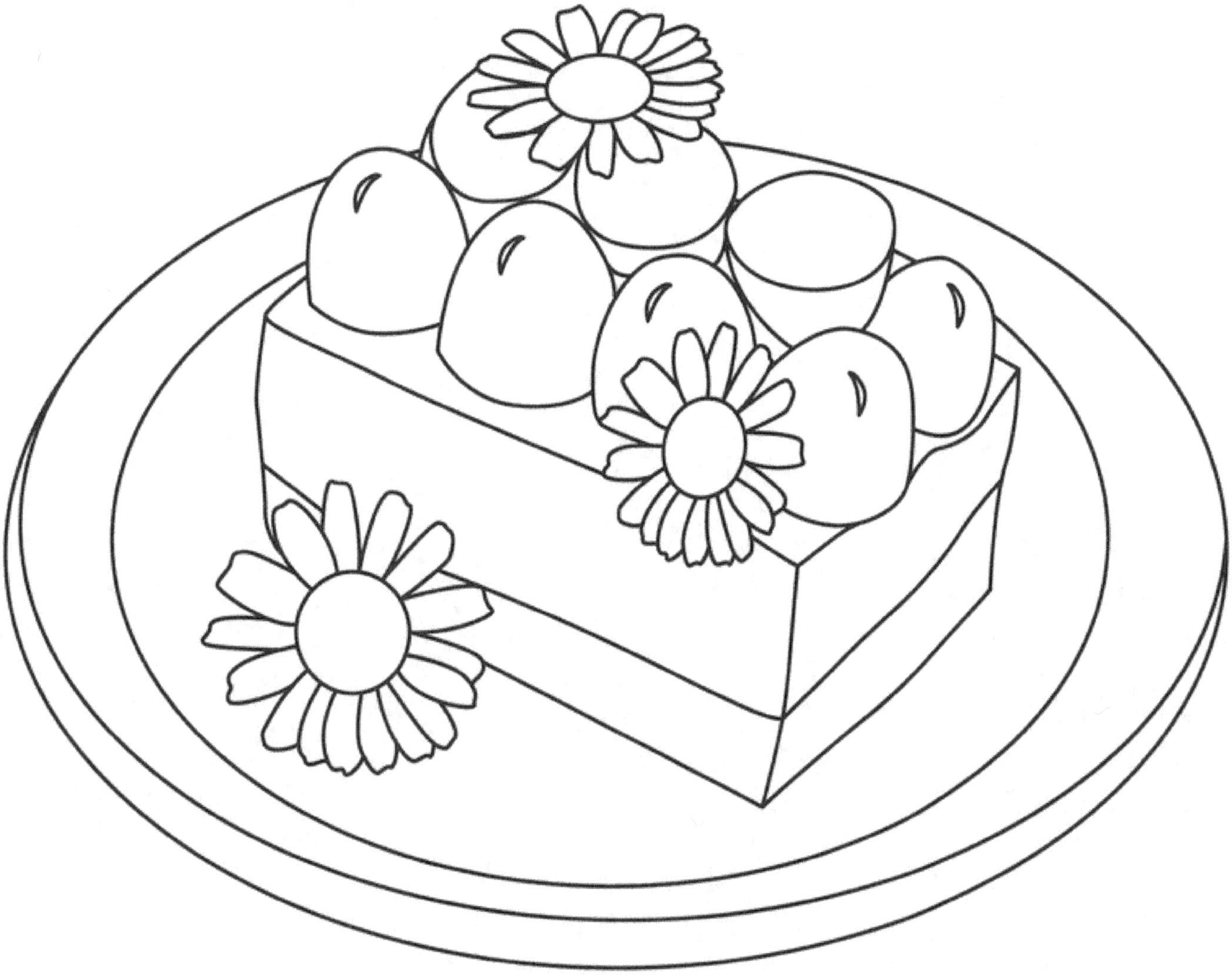

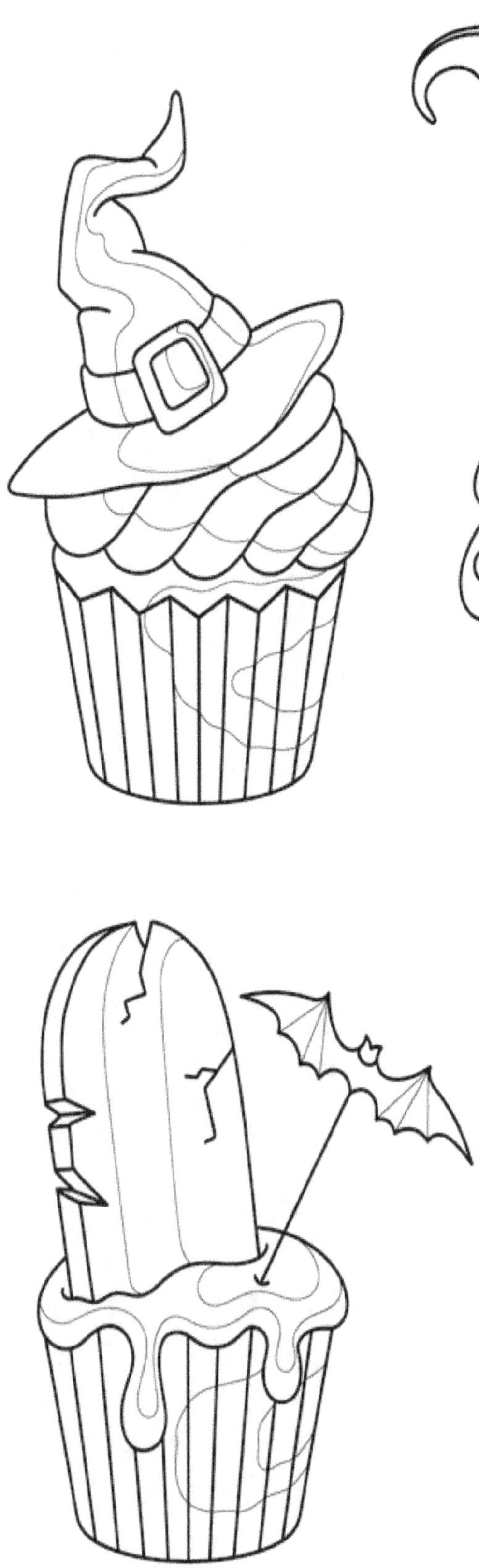

CAKE

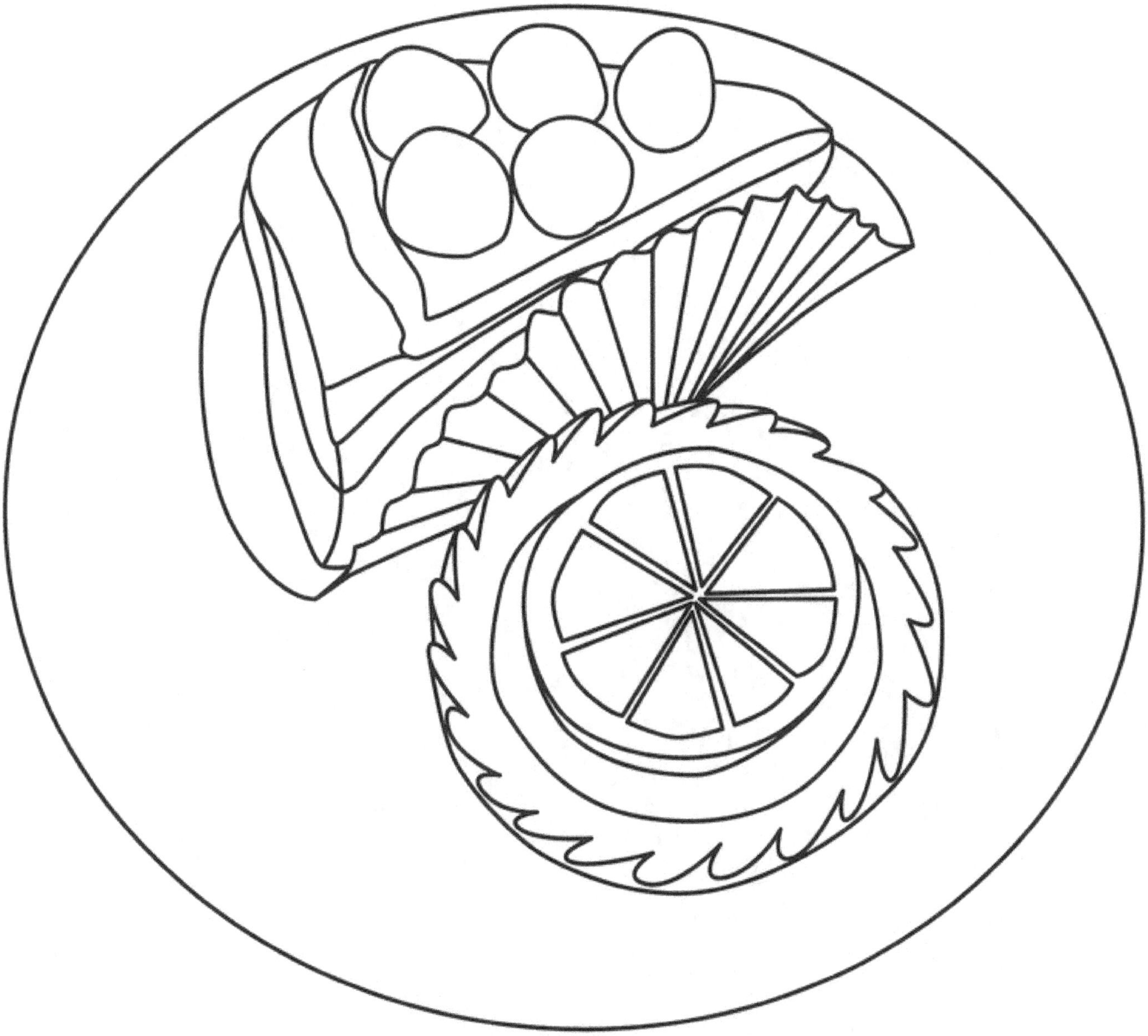

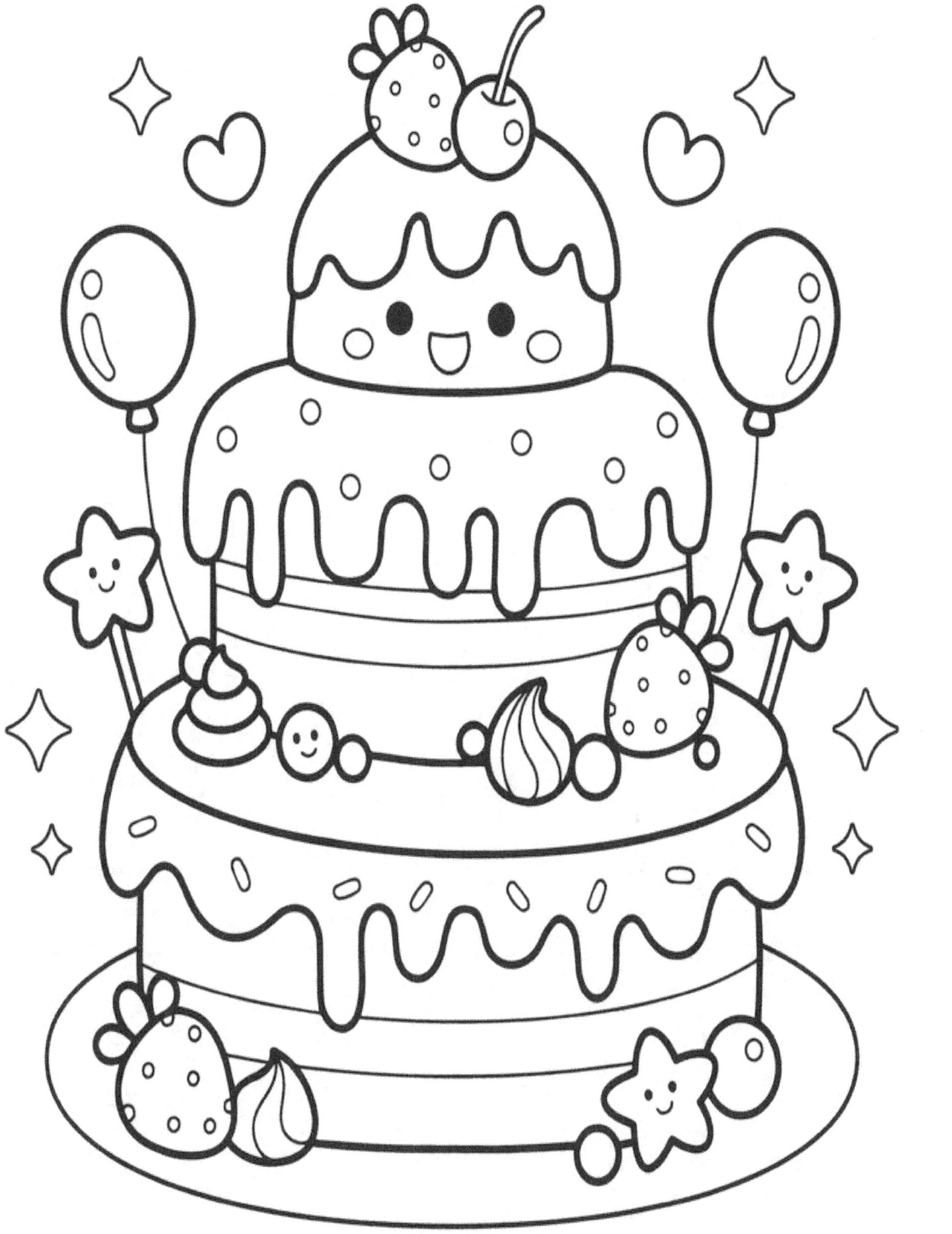

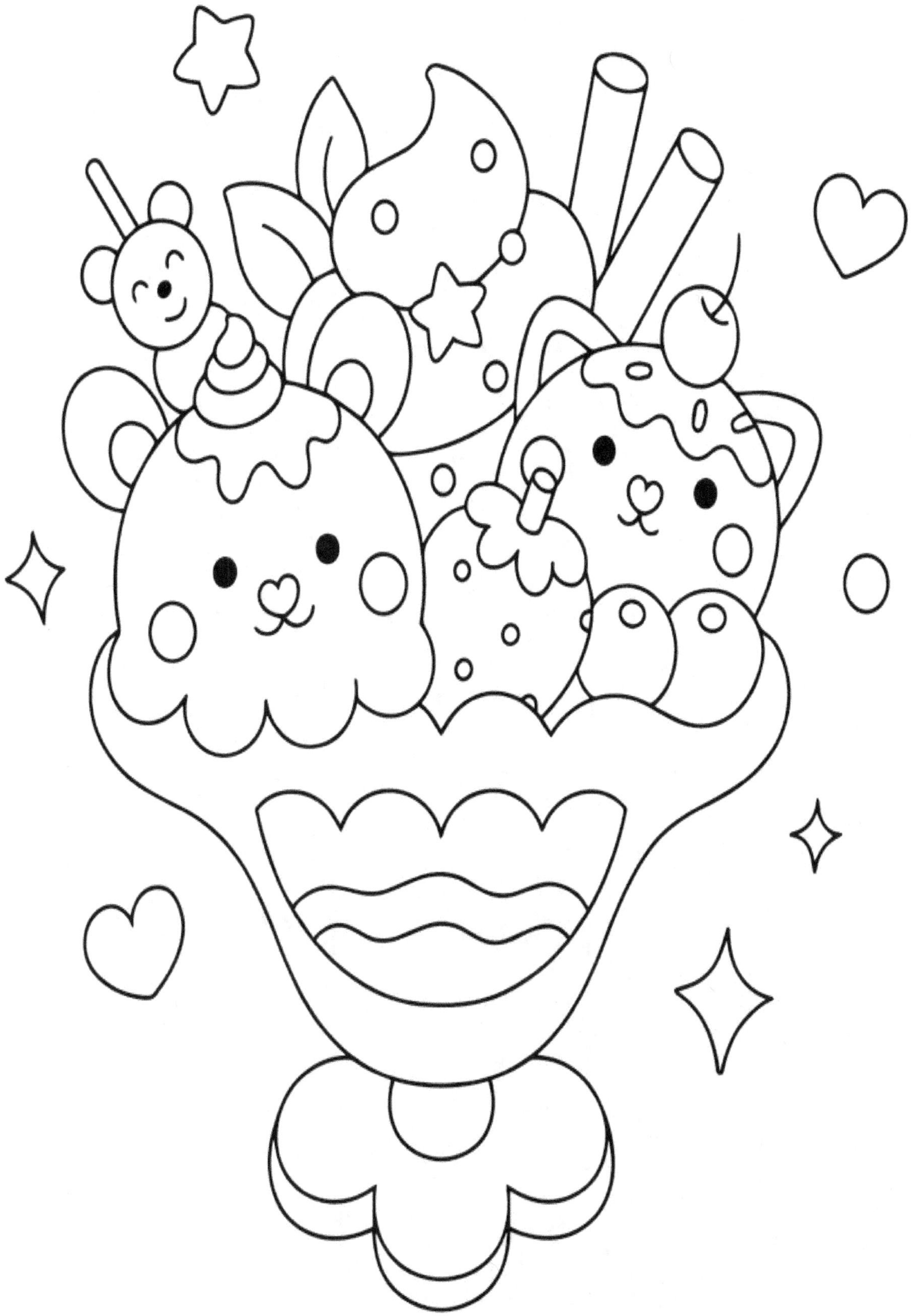

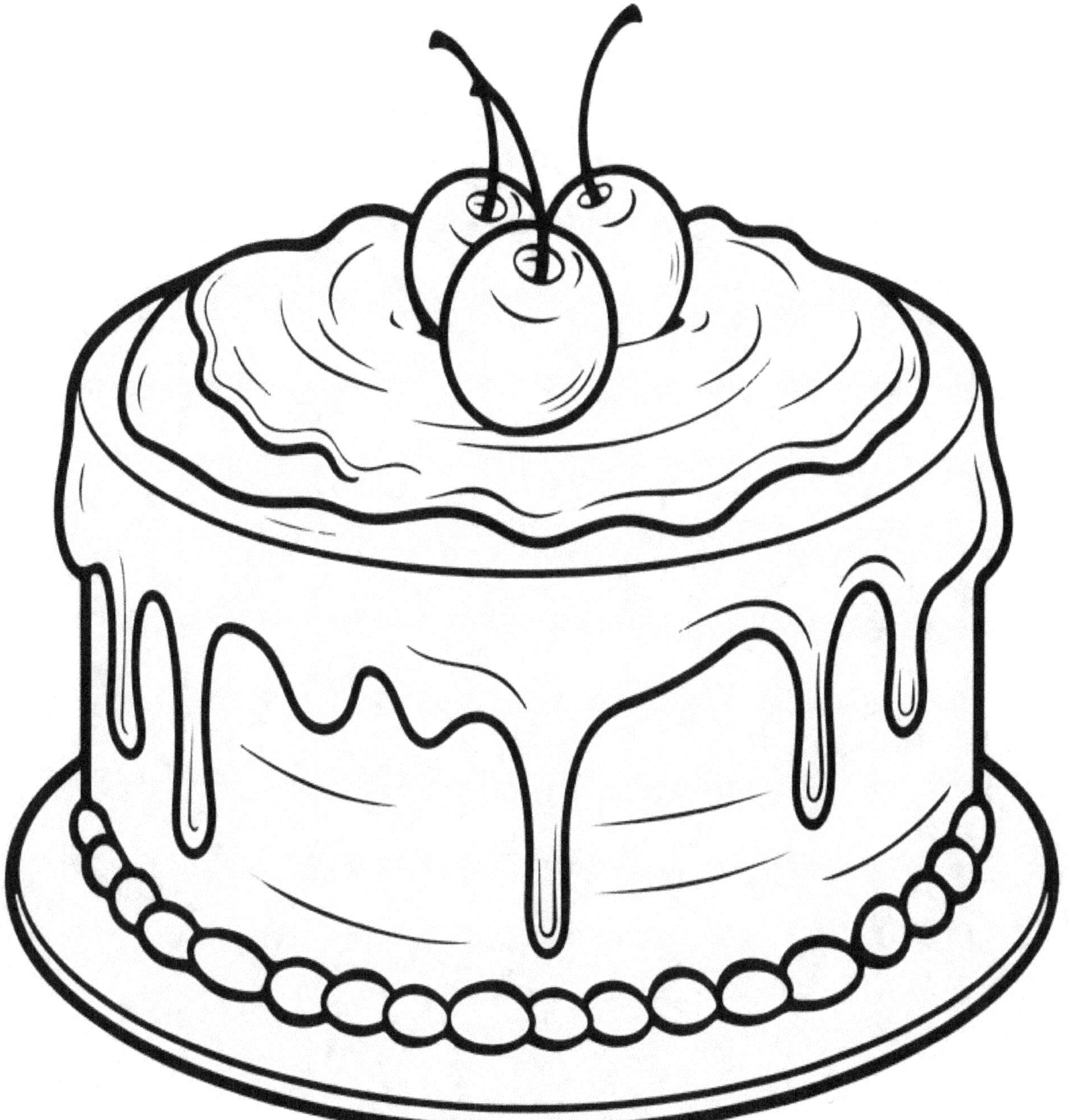

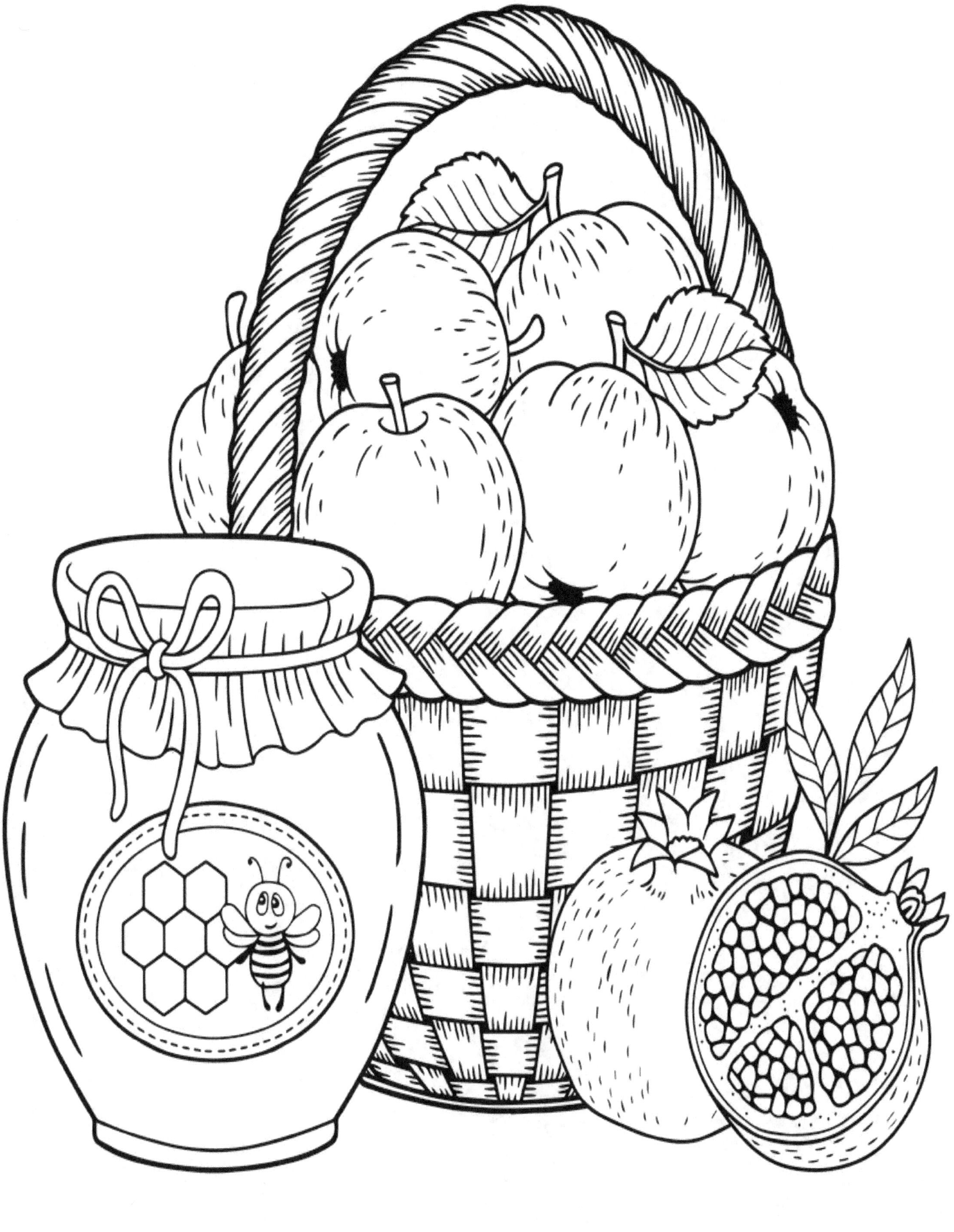

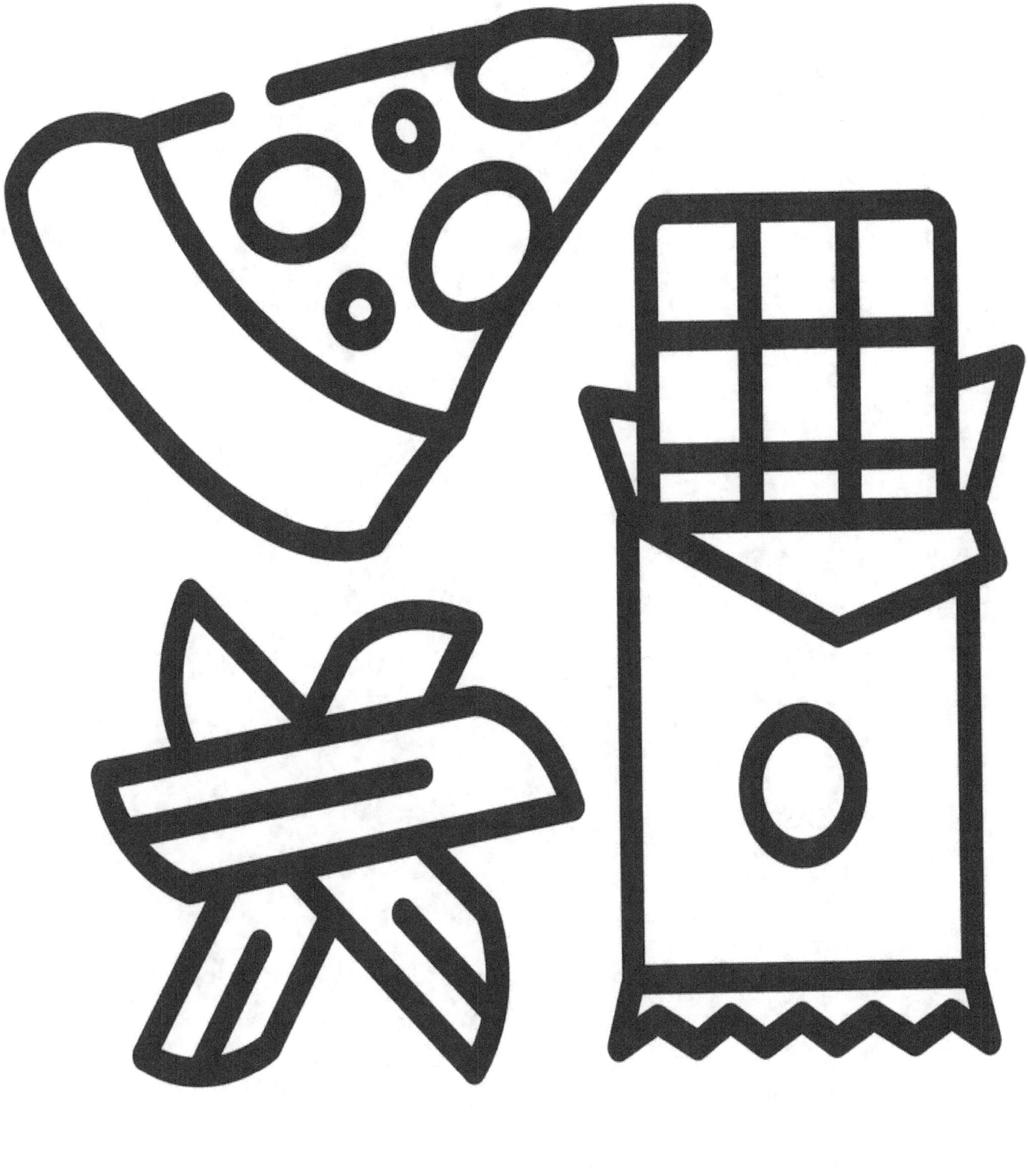

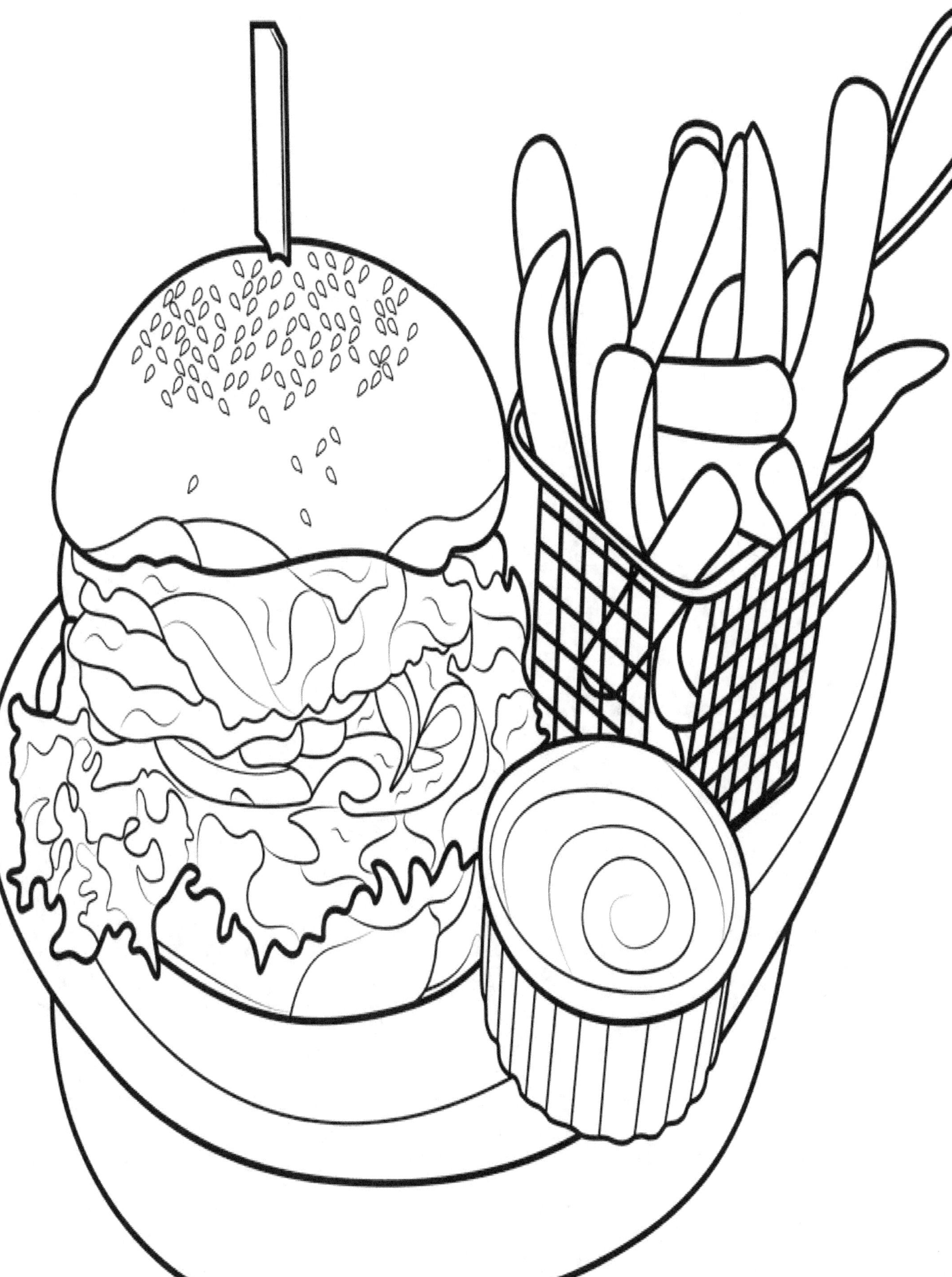

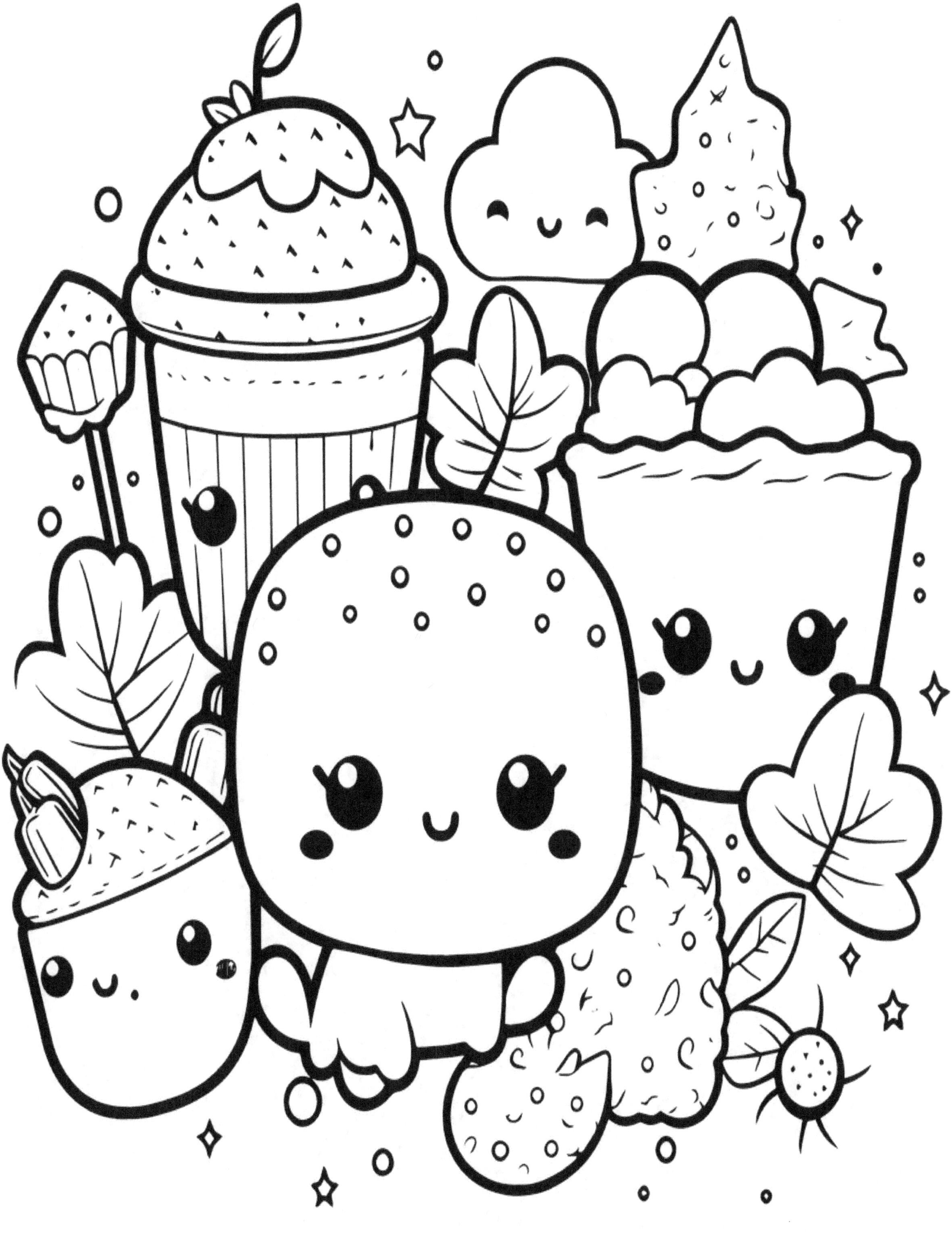

PANCAKE

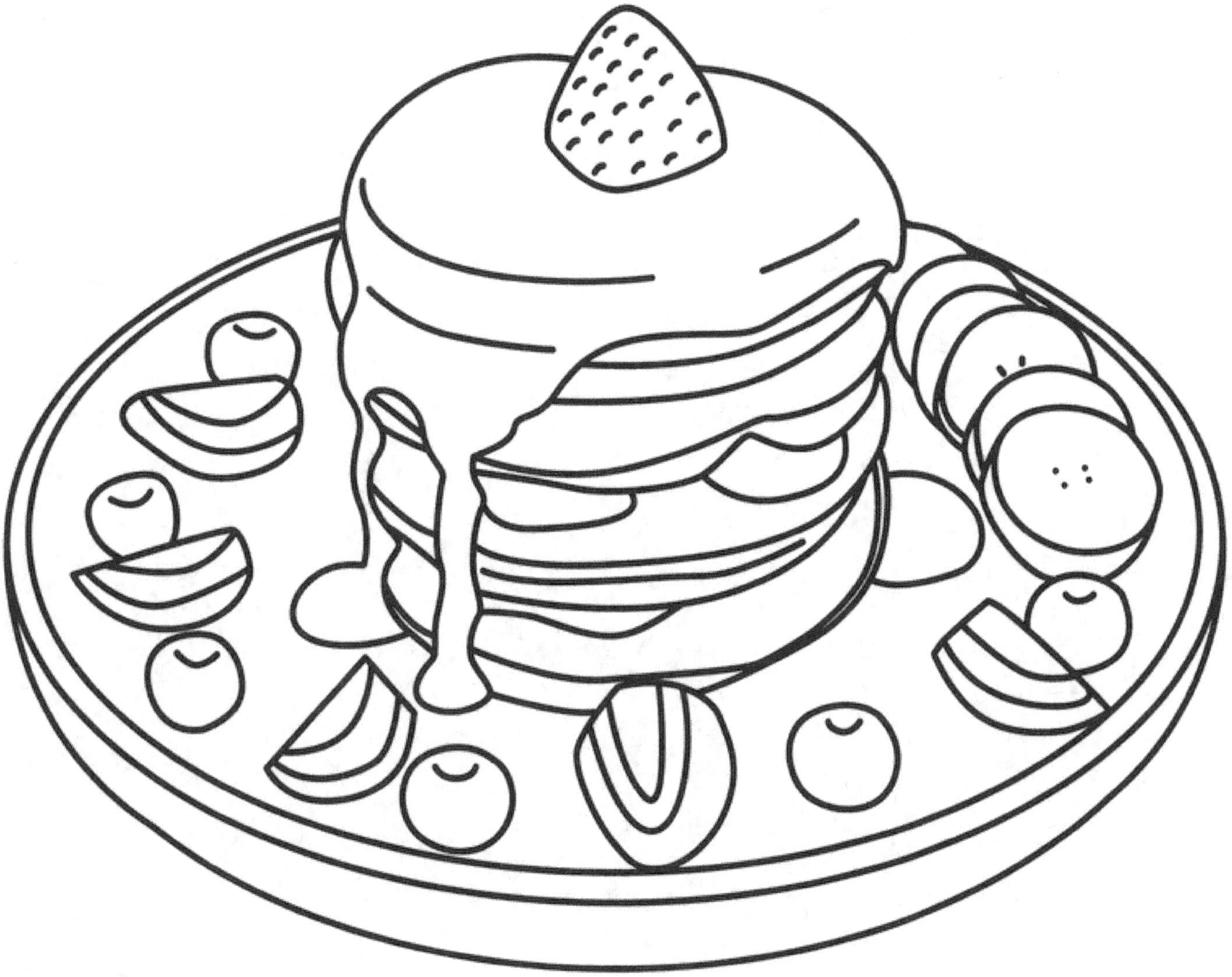

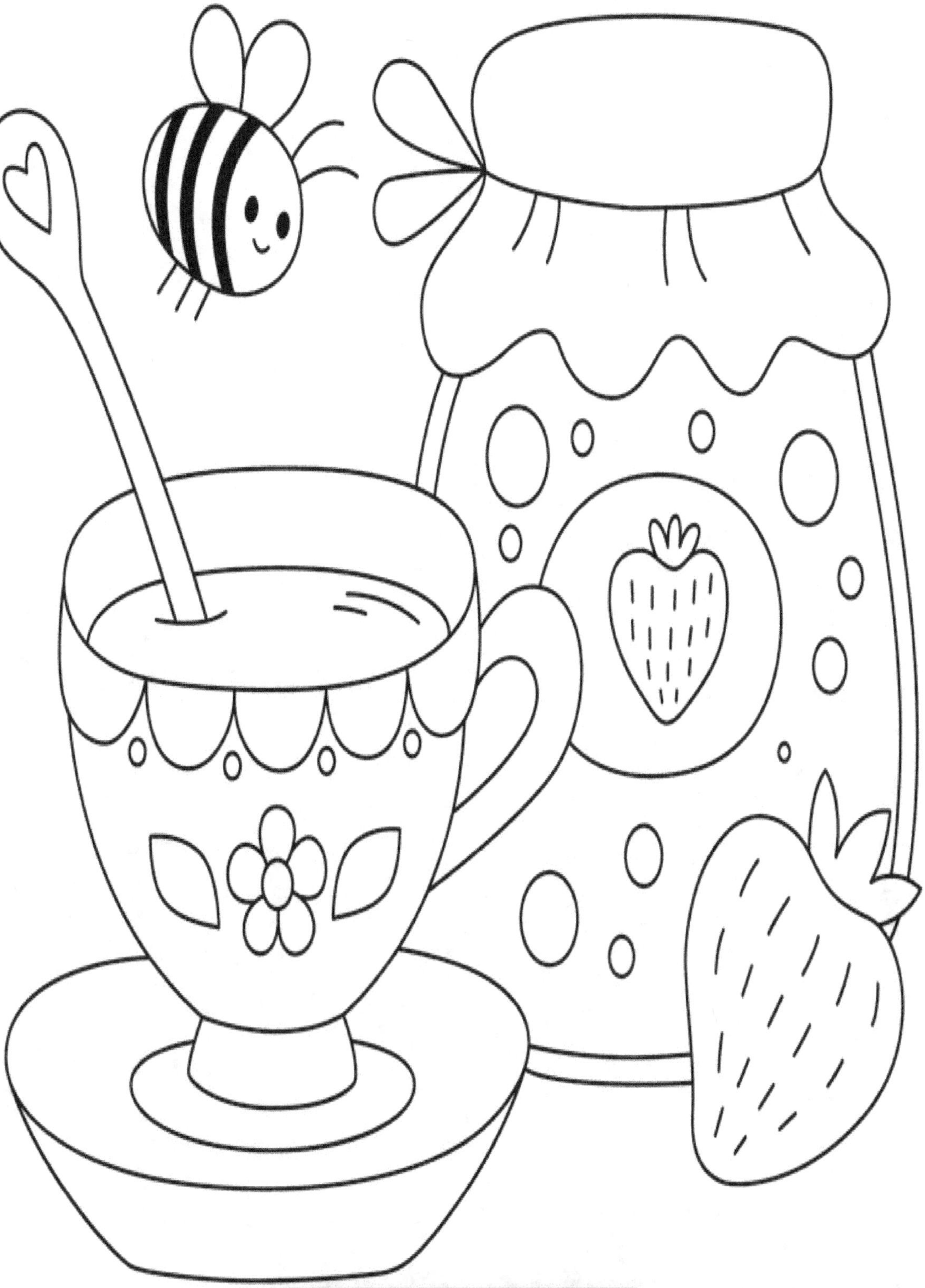

JAM

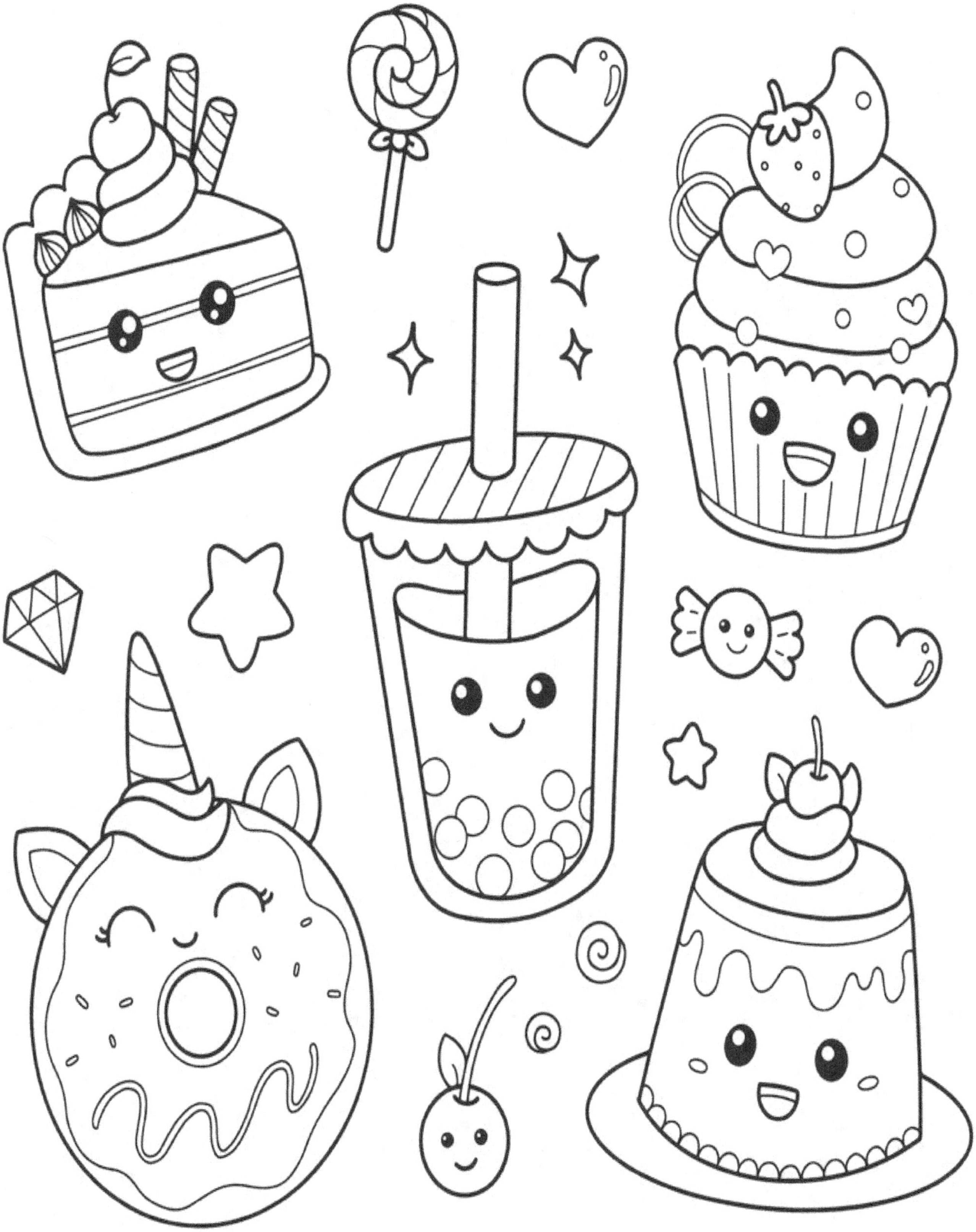

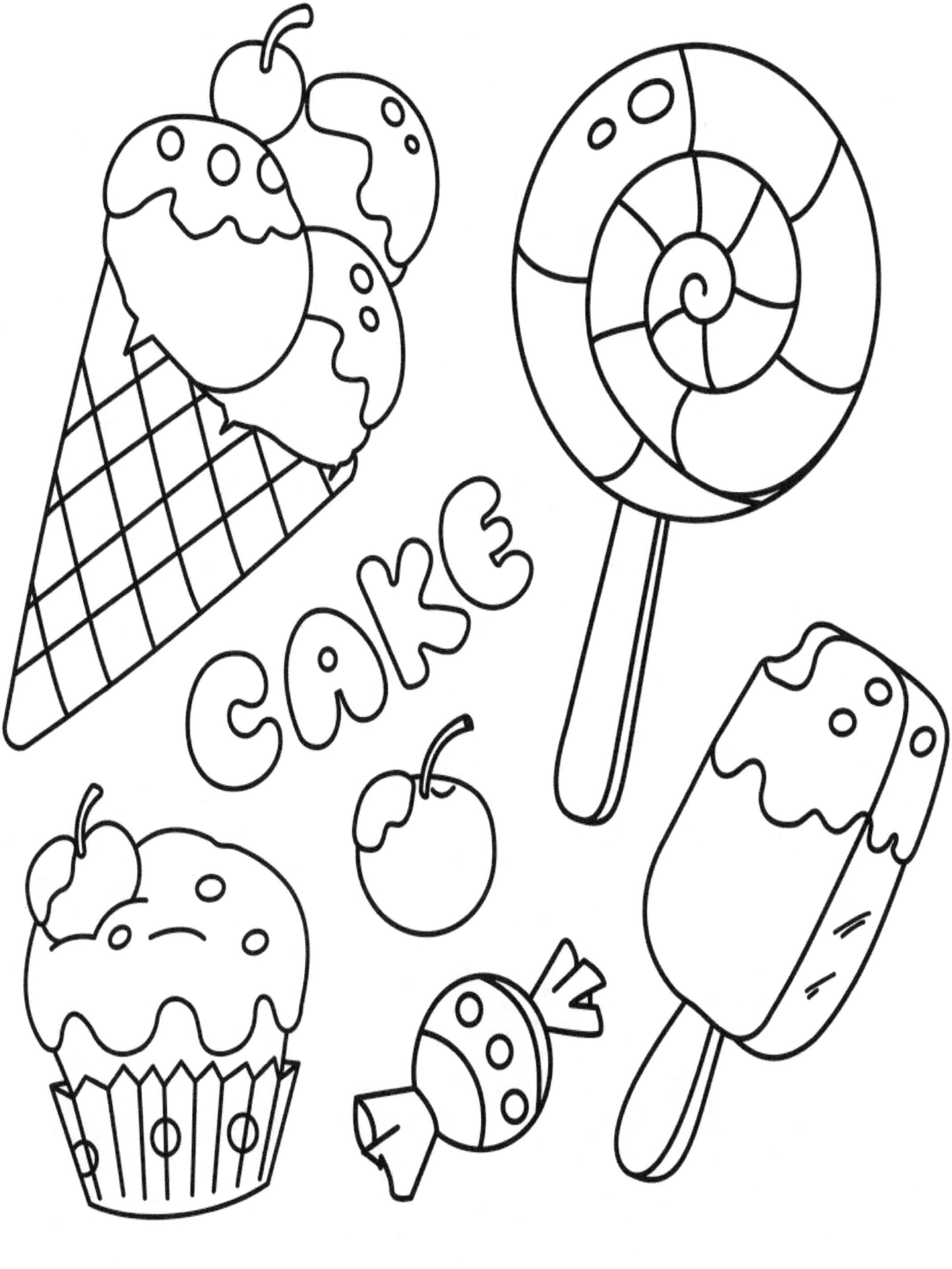
CAKE

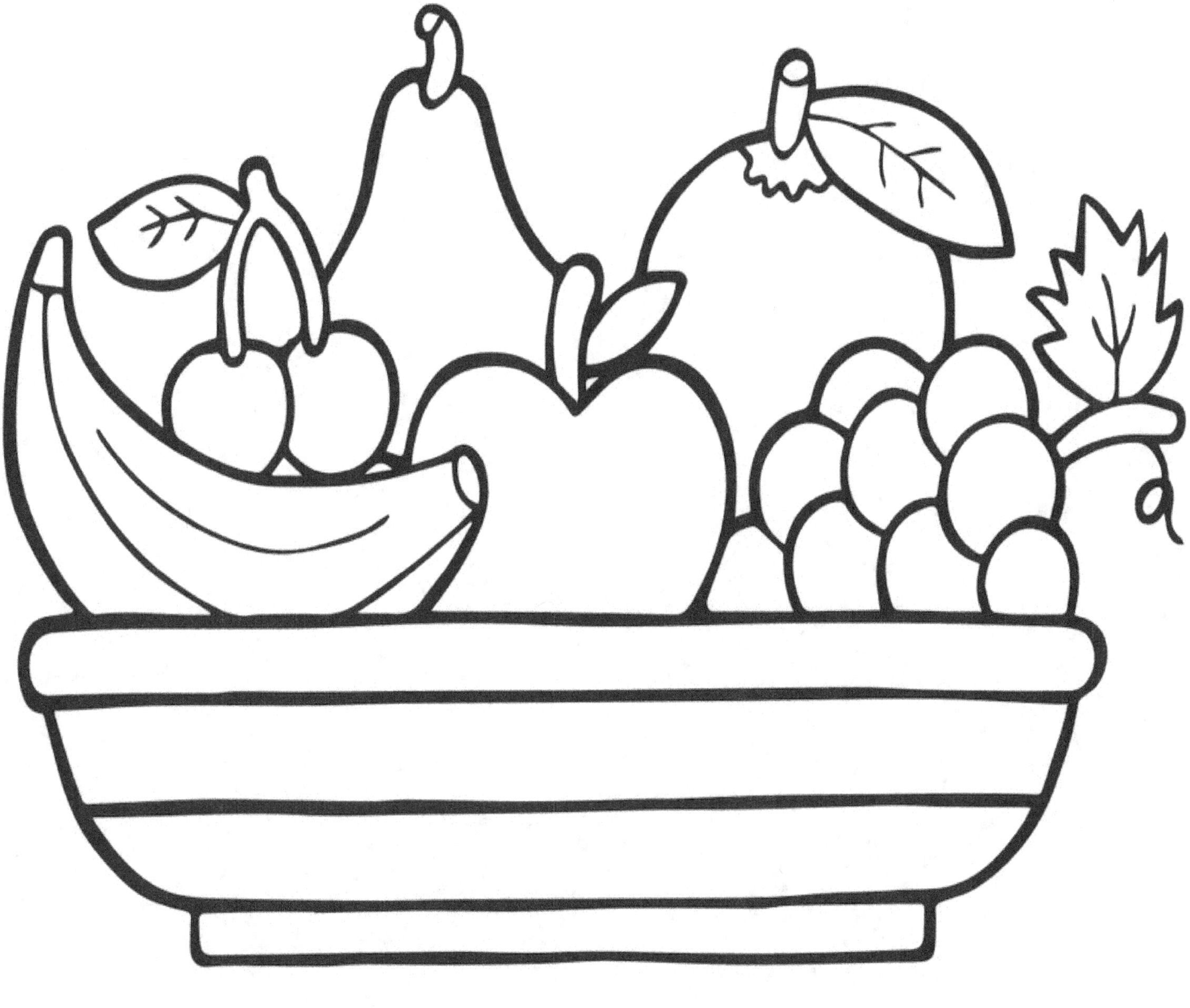

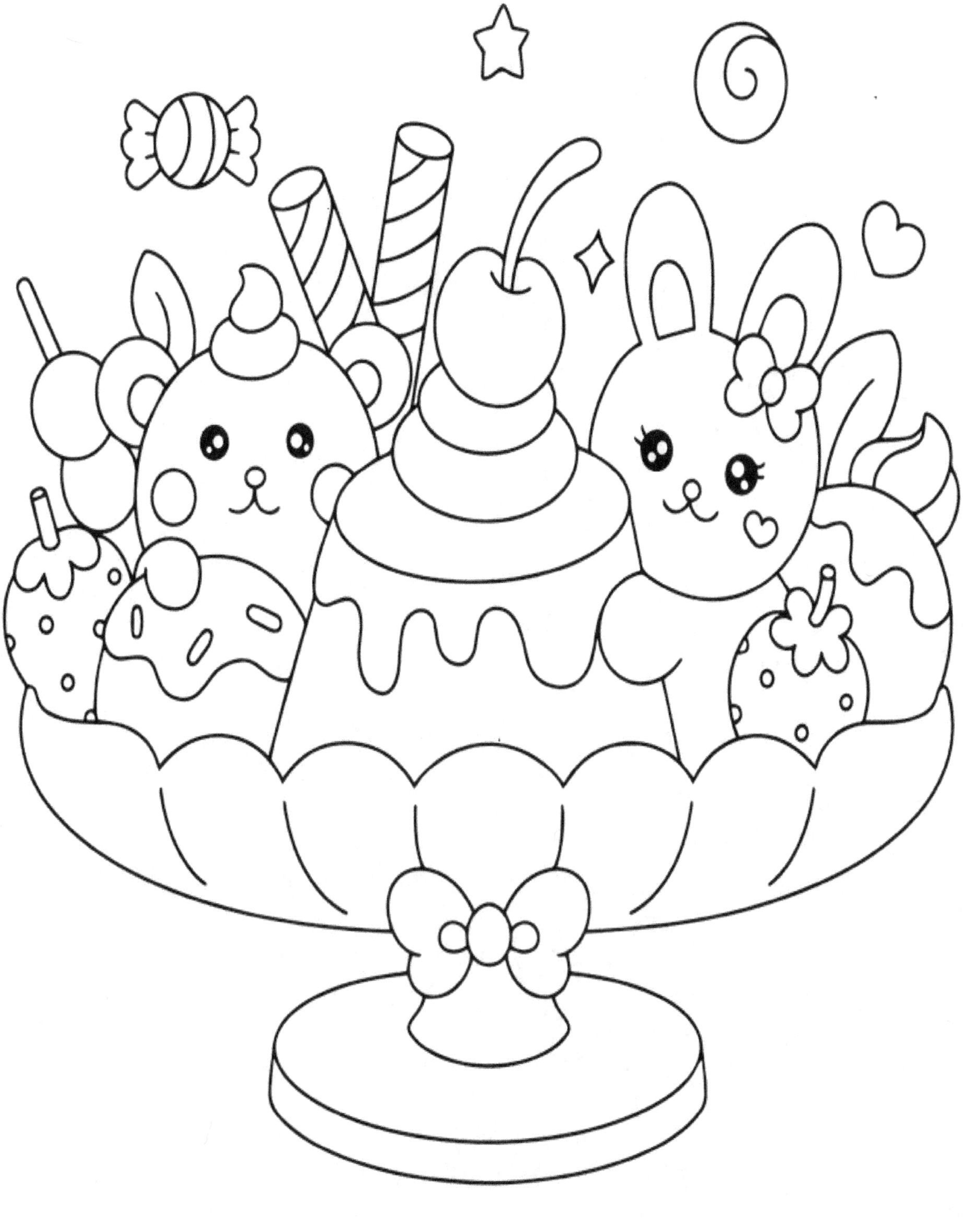

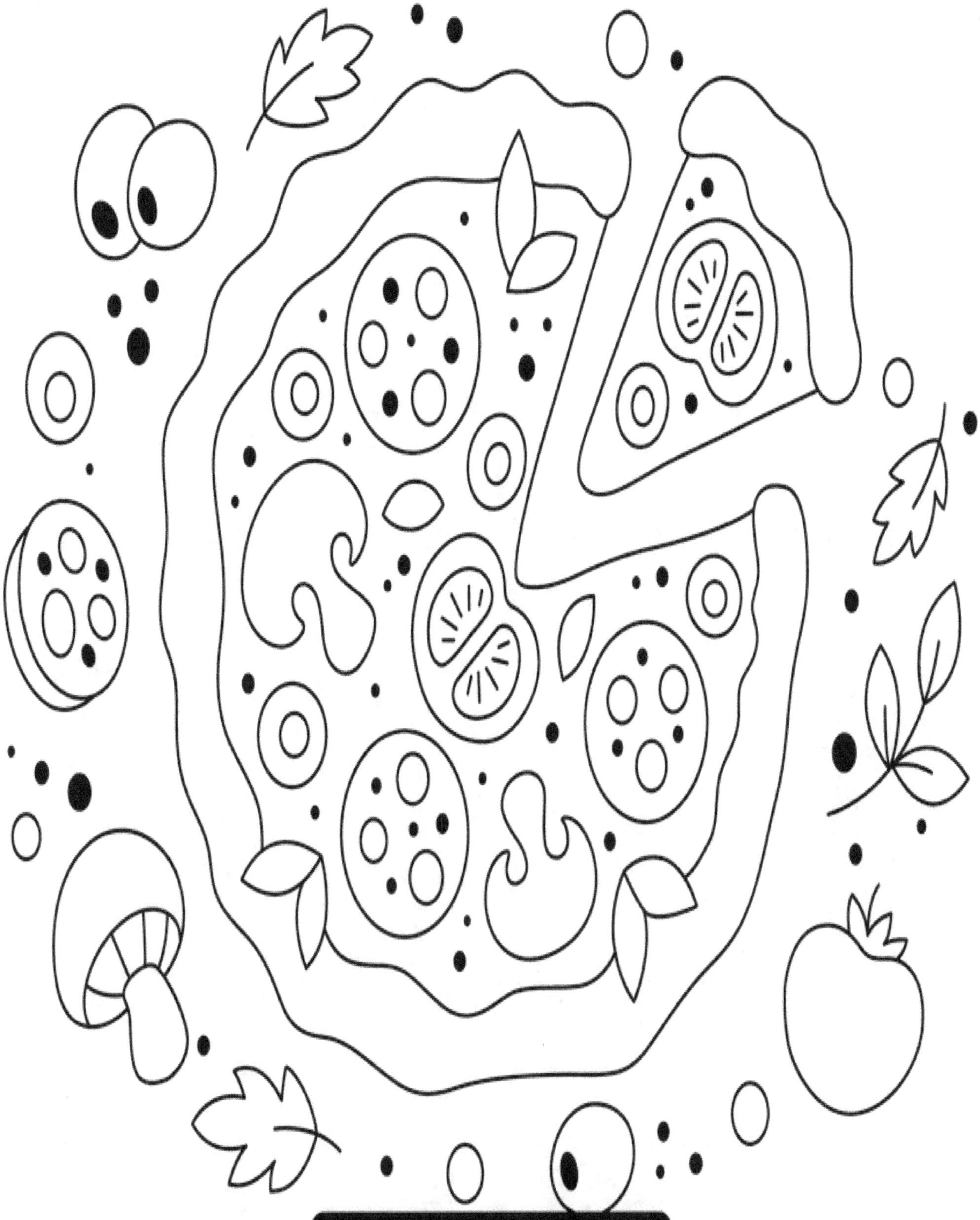

PIZZA

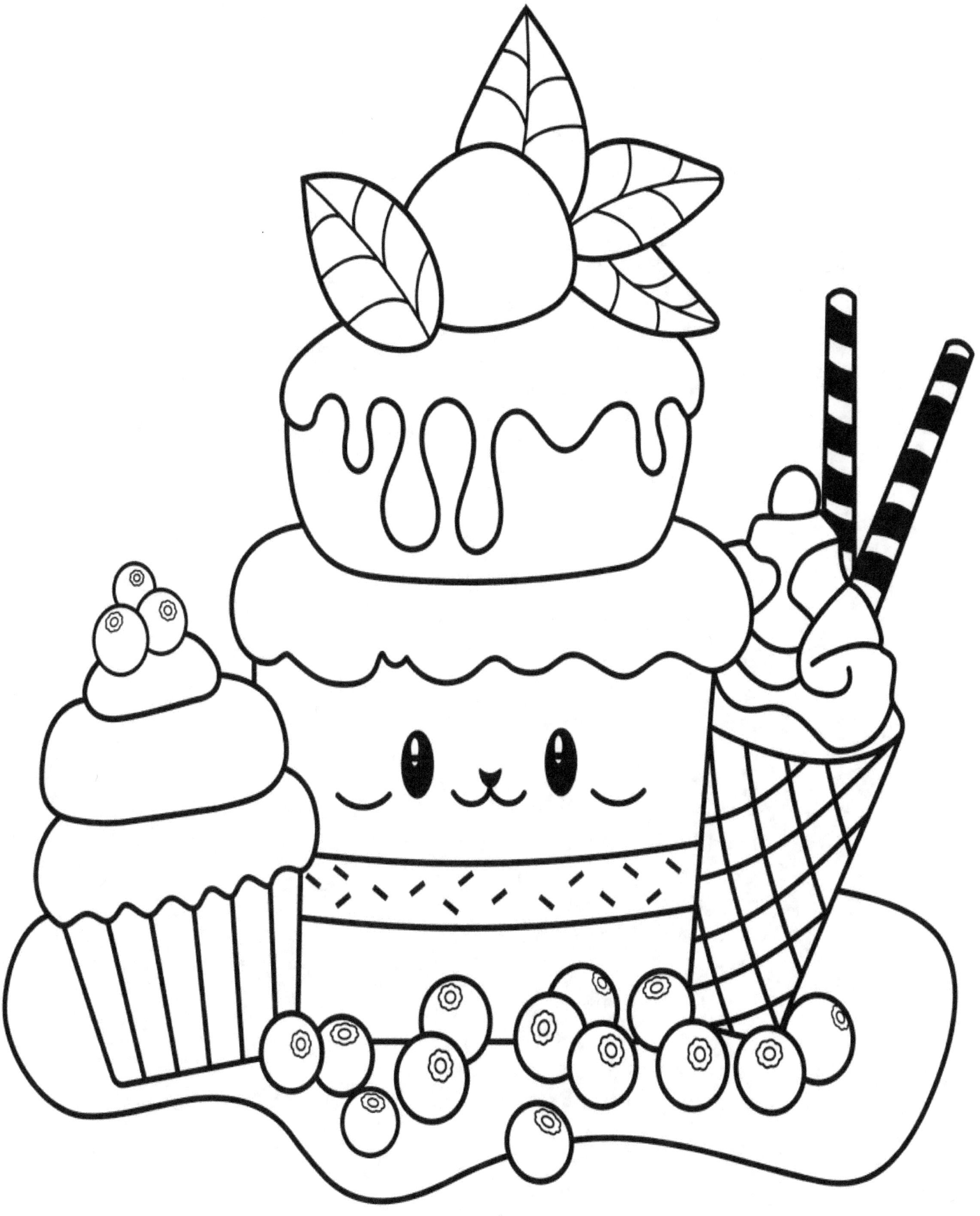

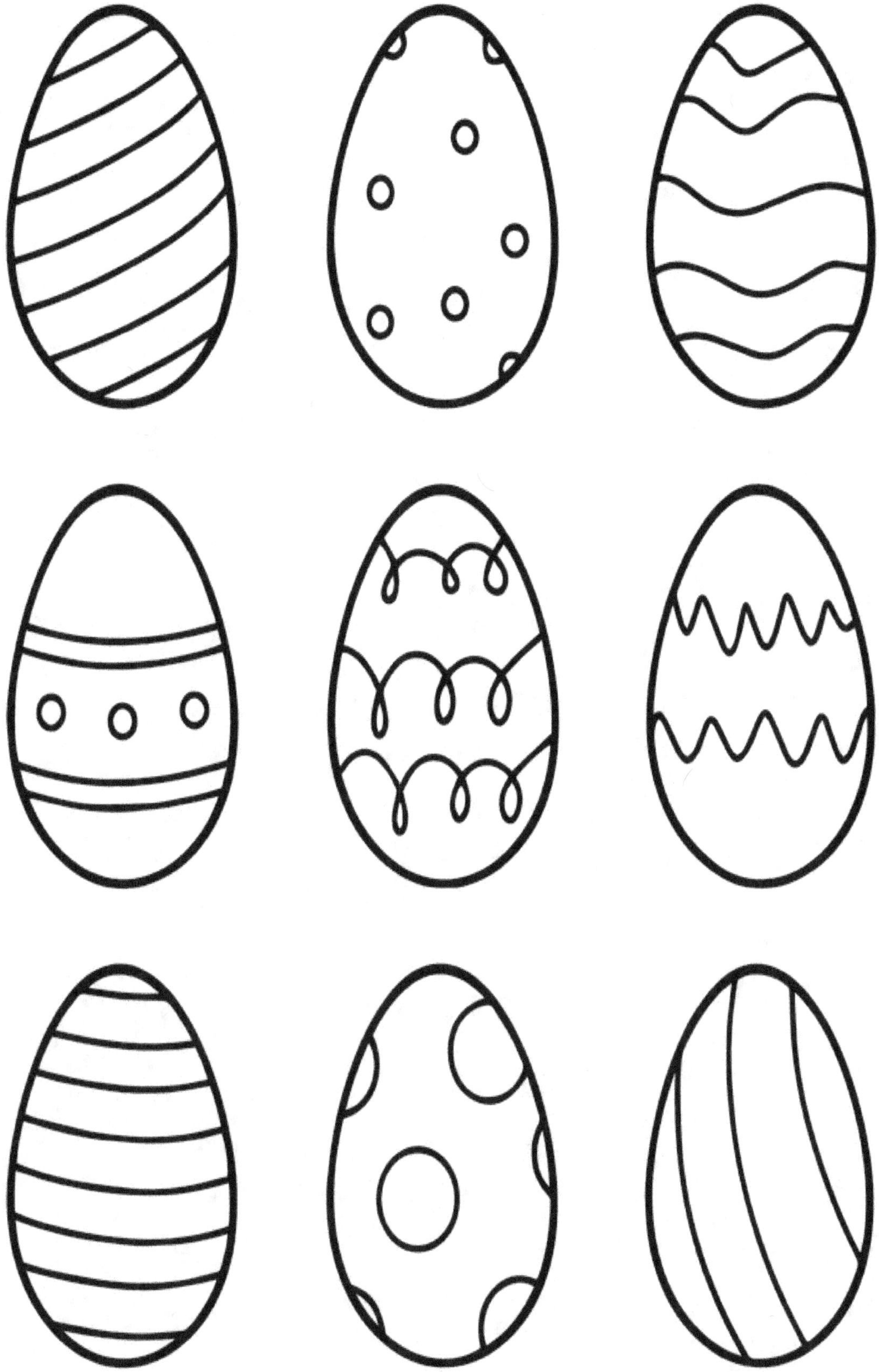

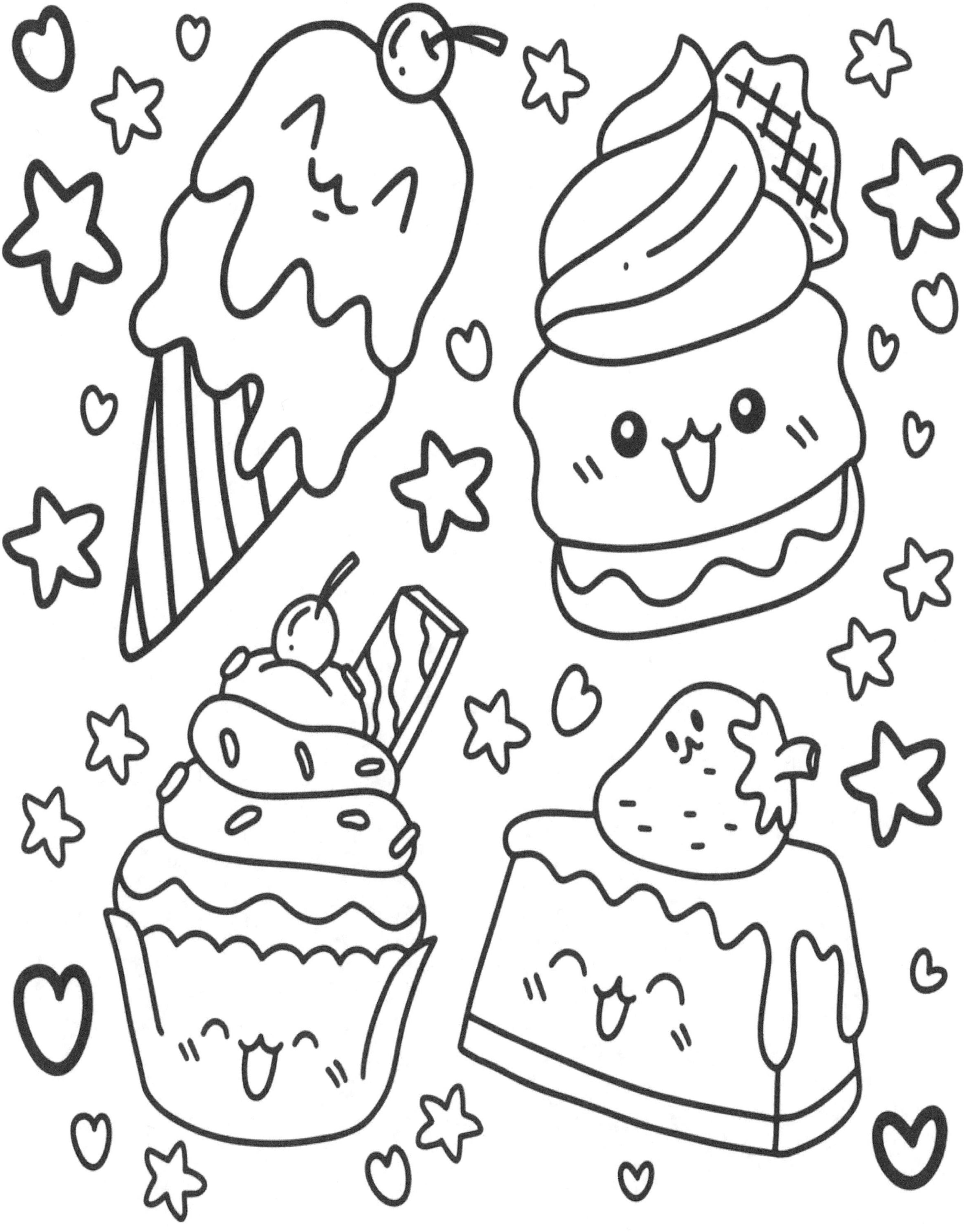

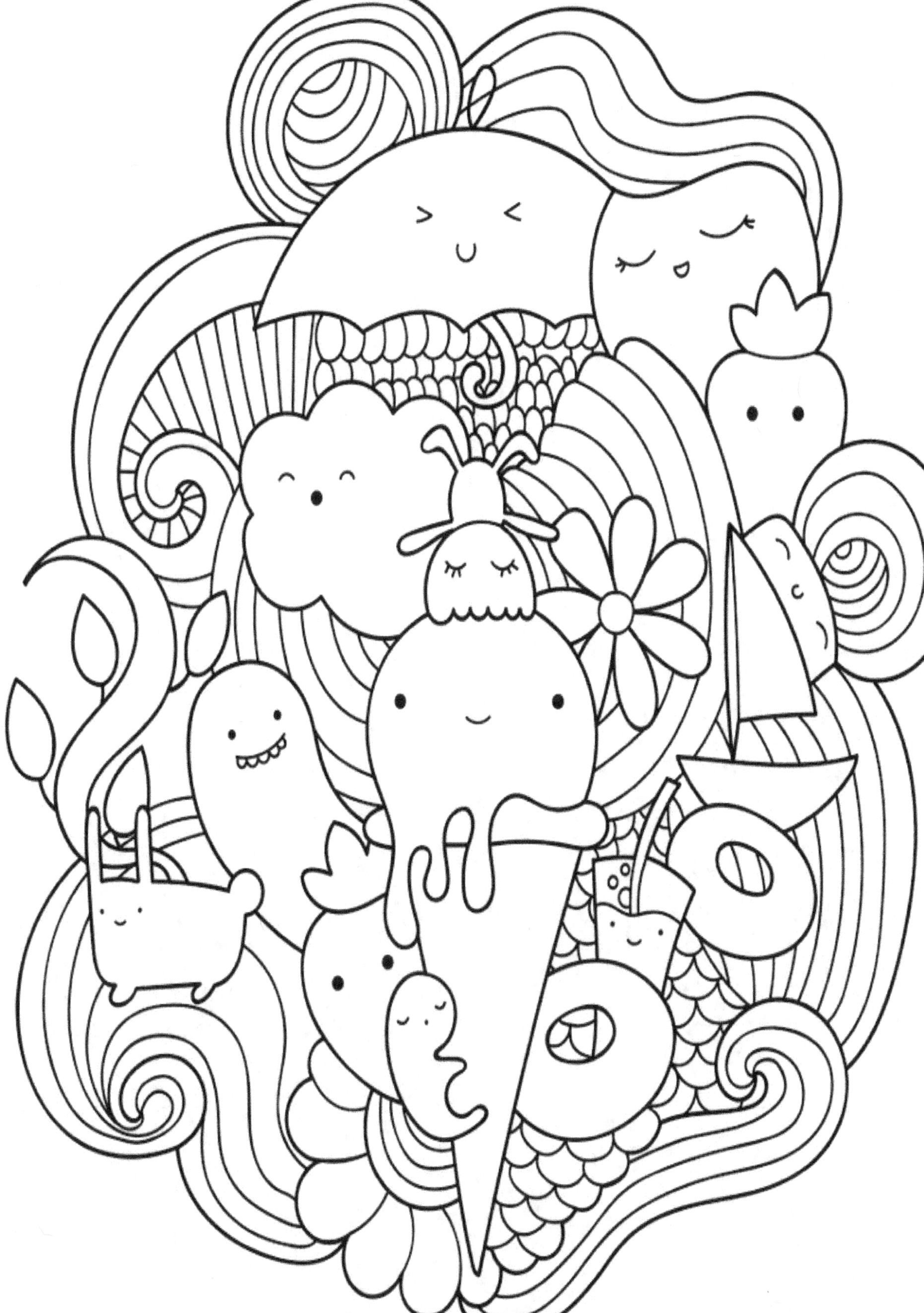

ROLL CAKE

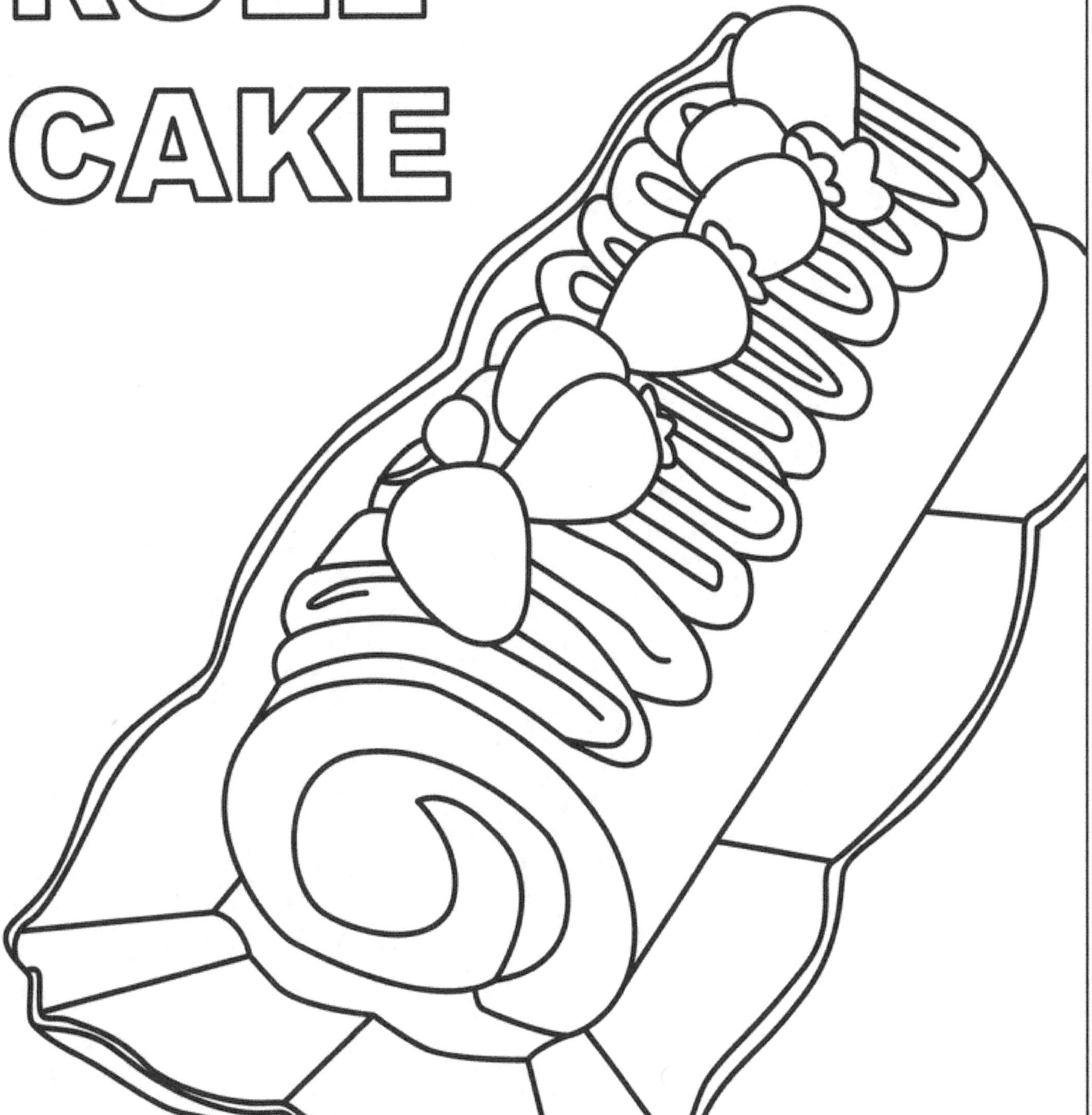

MILK
Yogurt

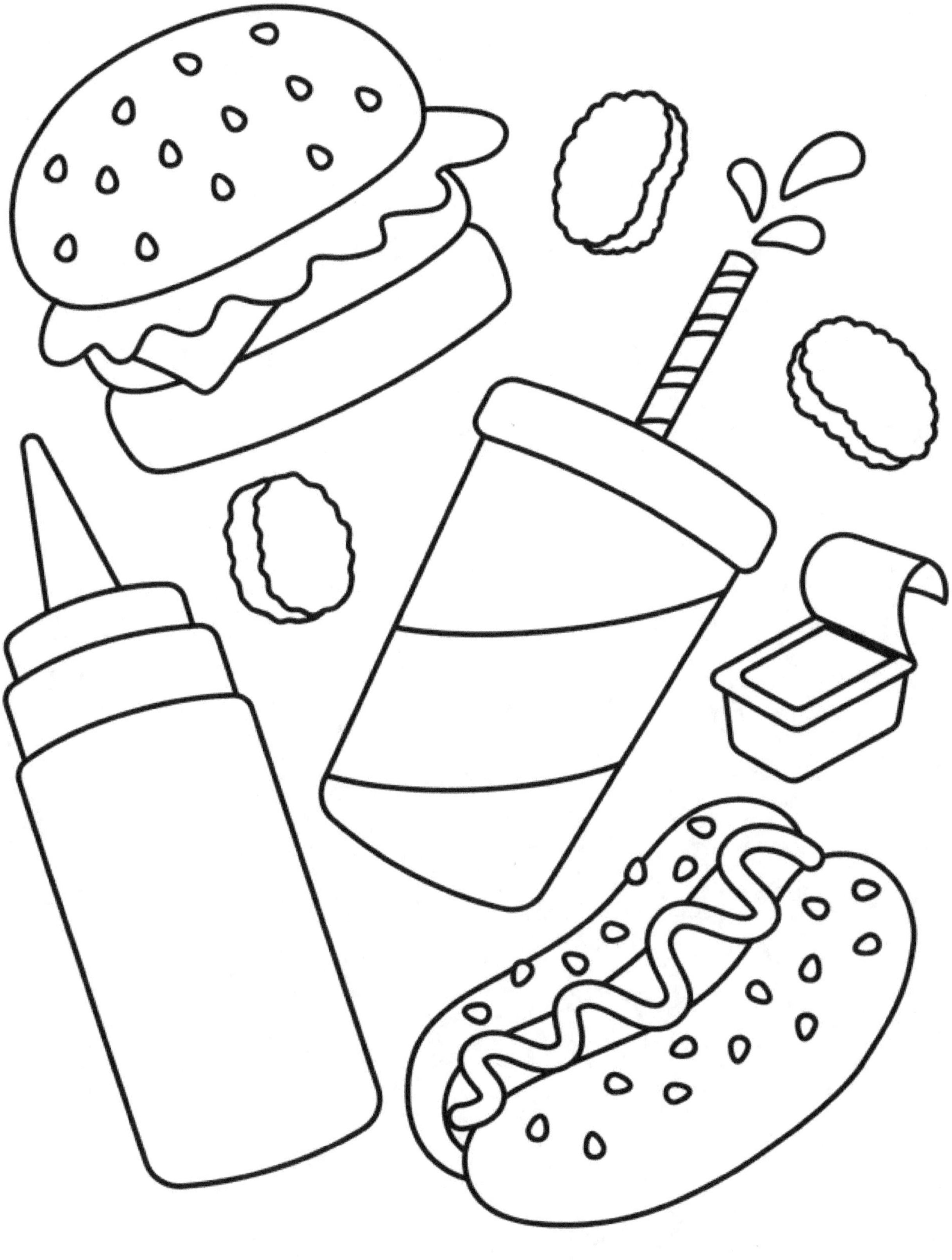

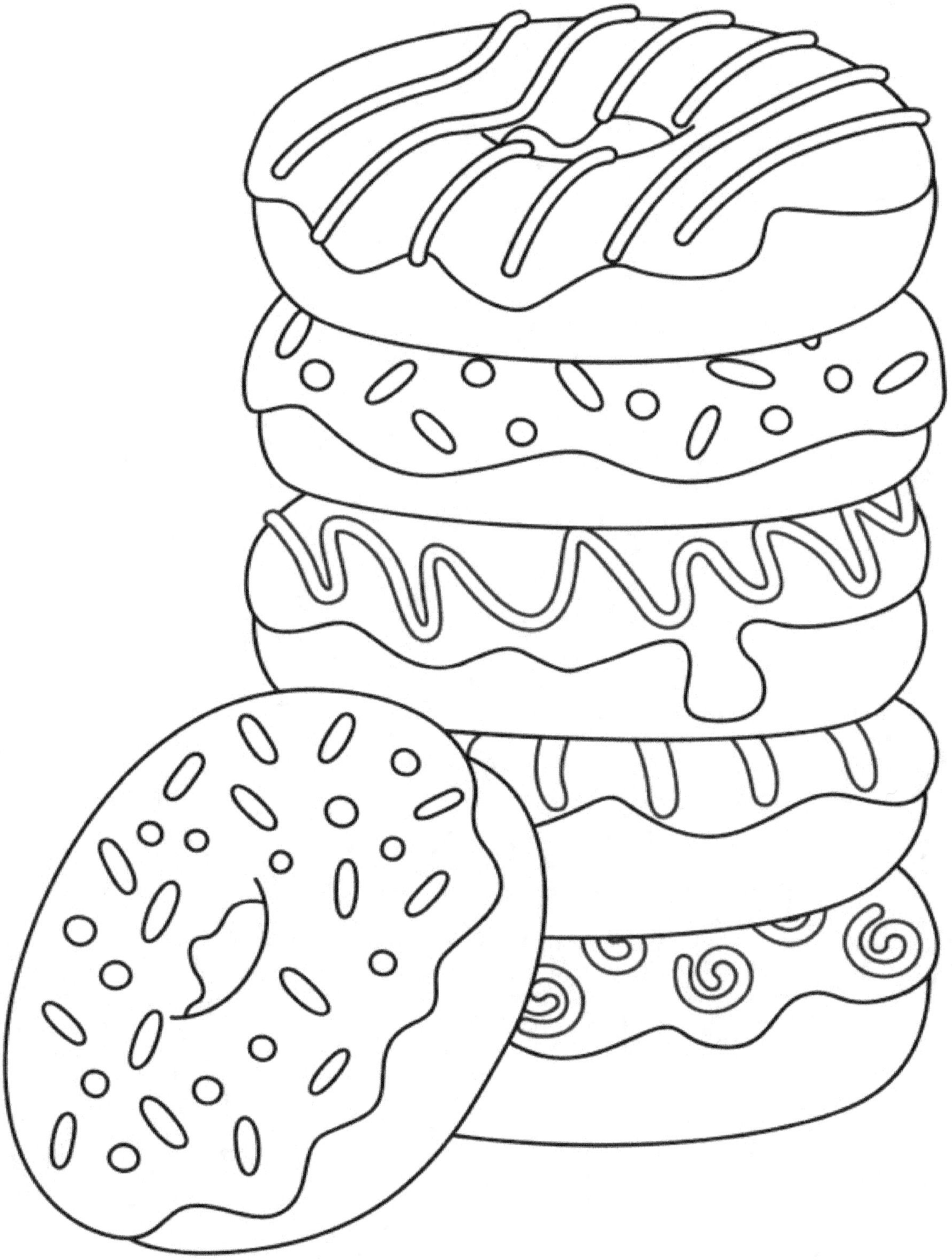

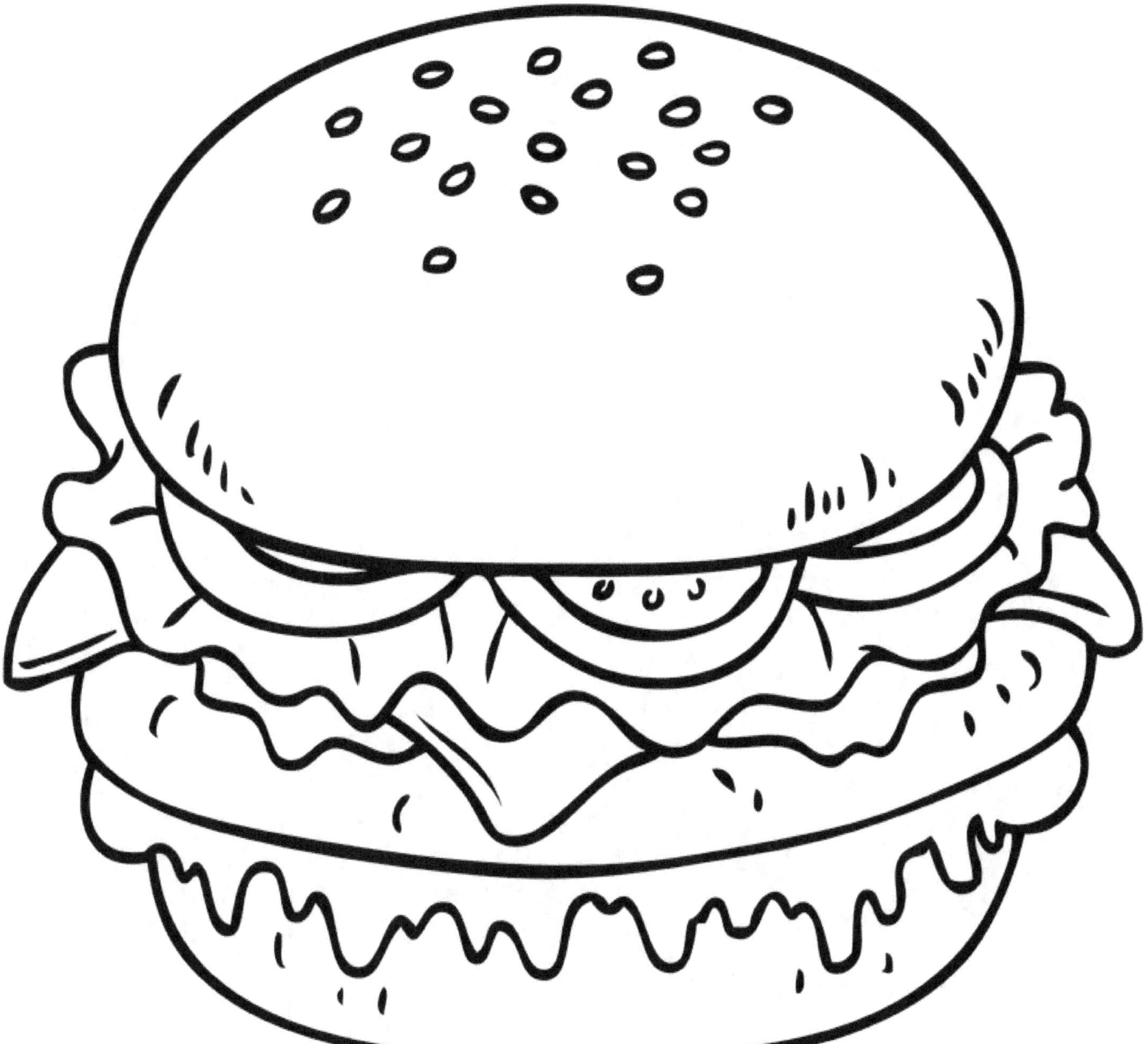

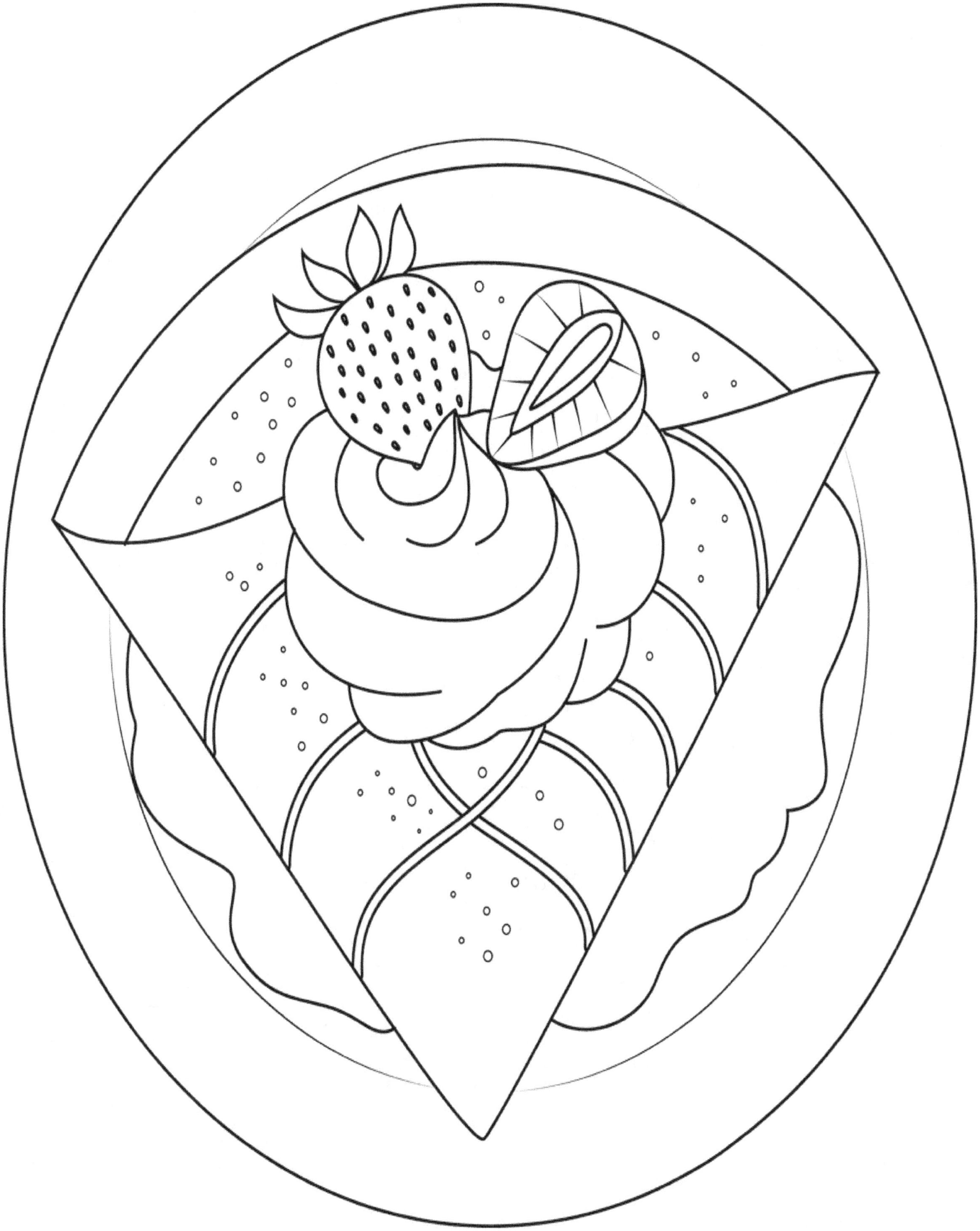

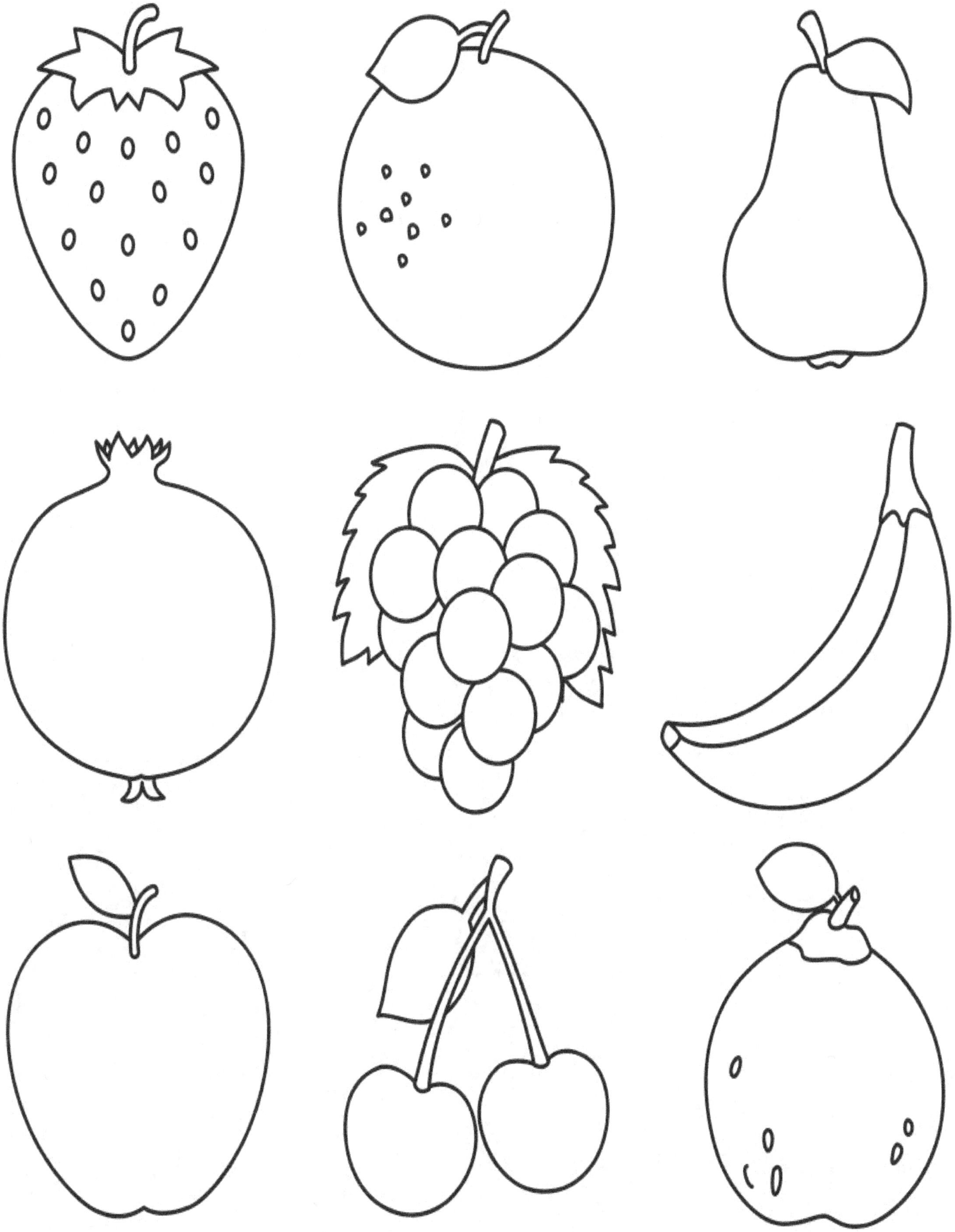

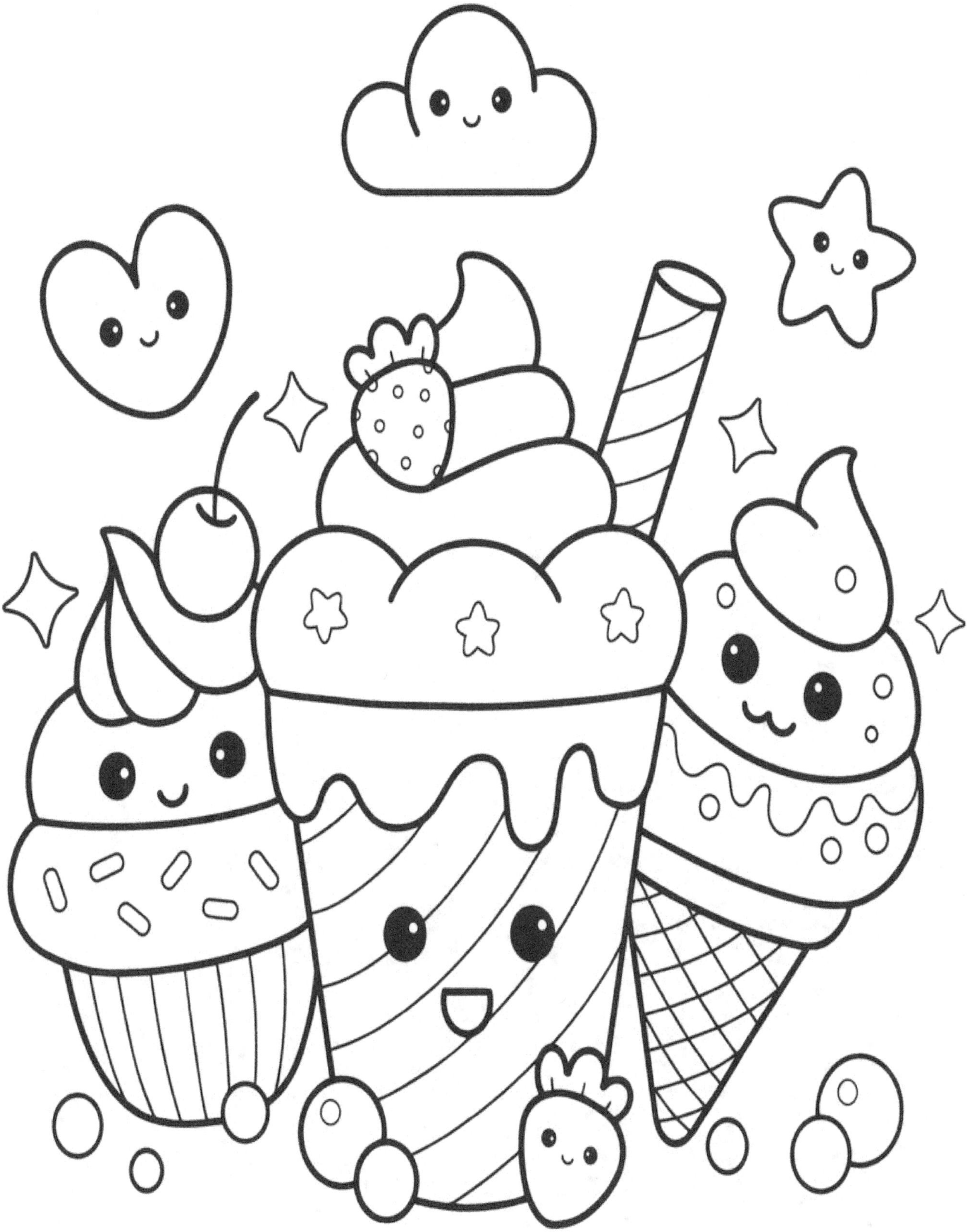

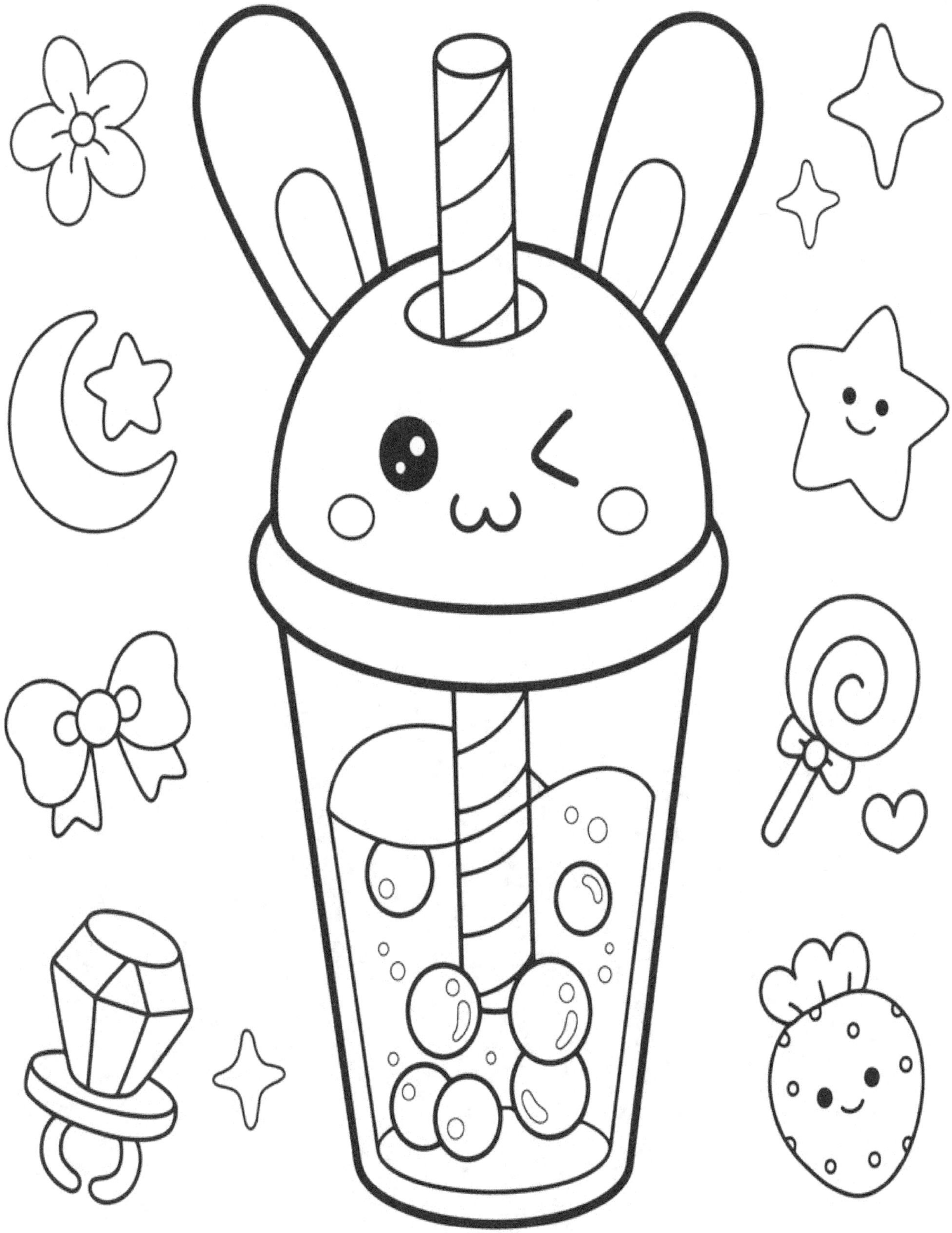

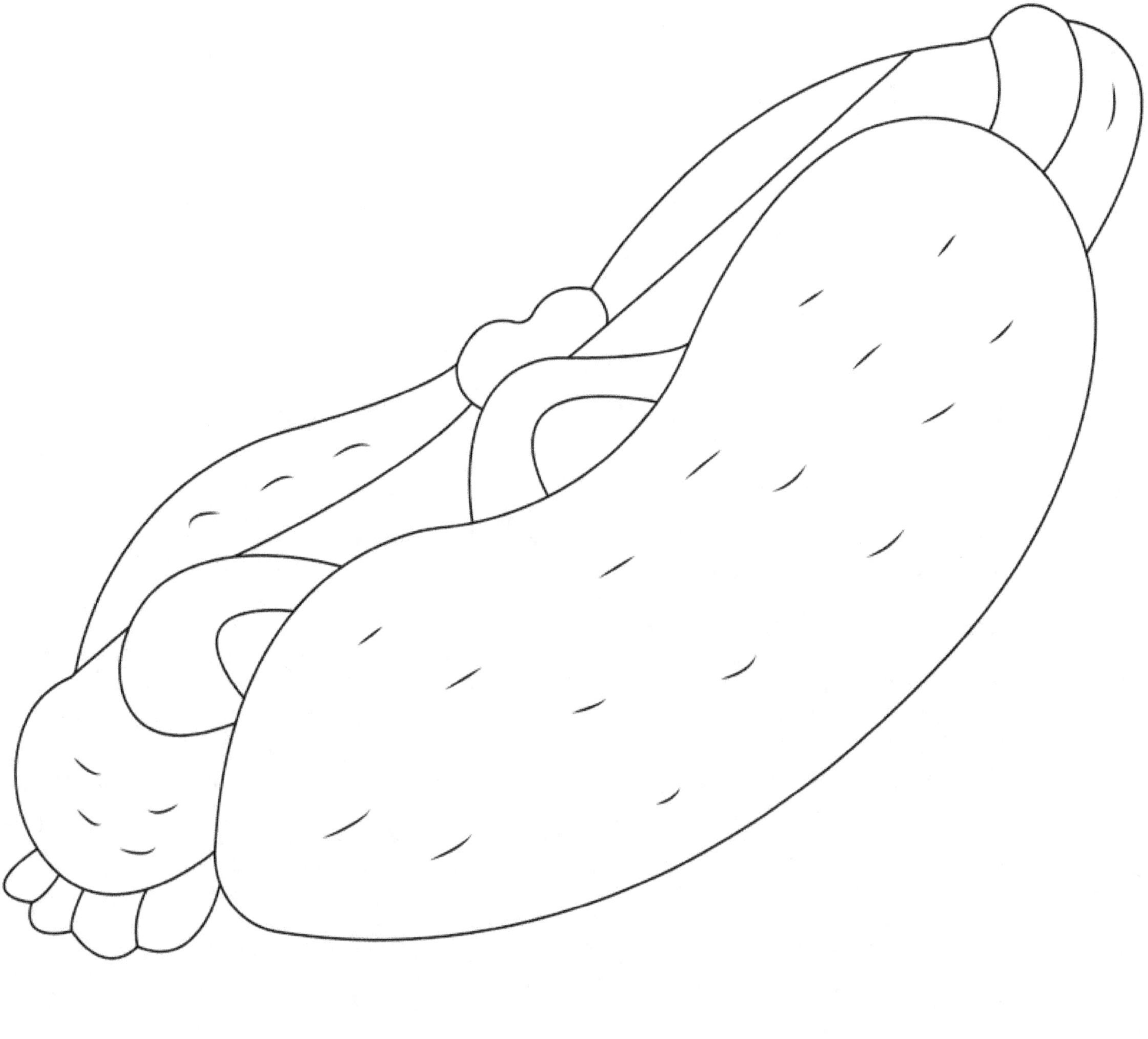

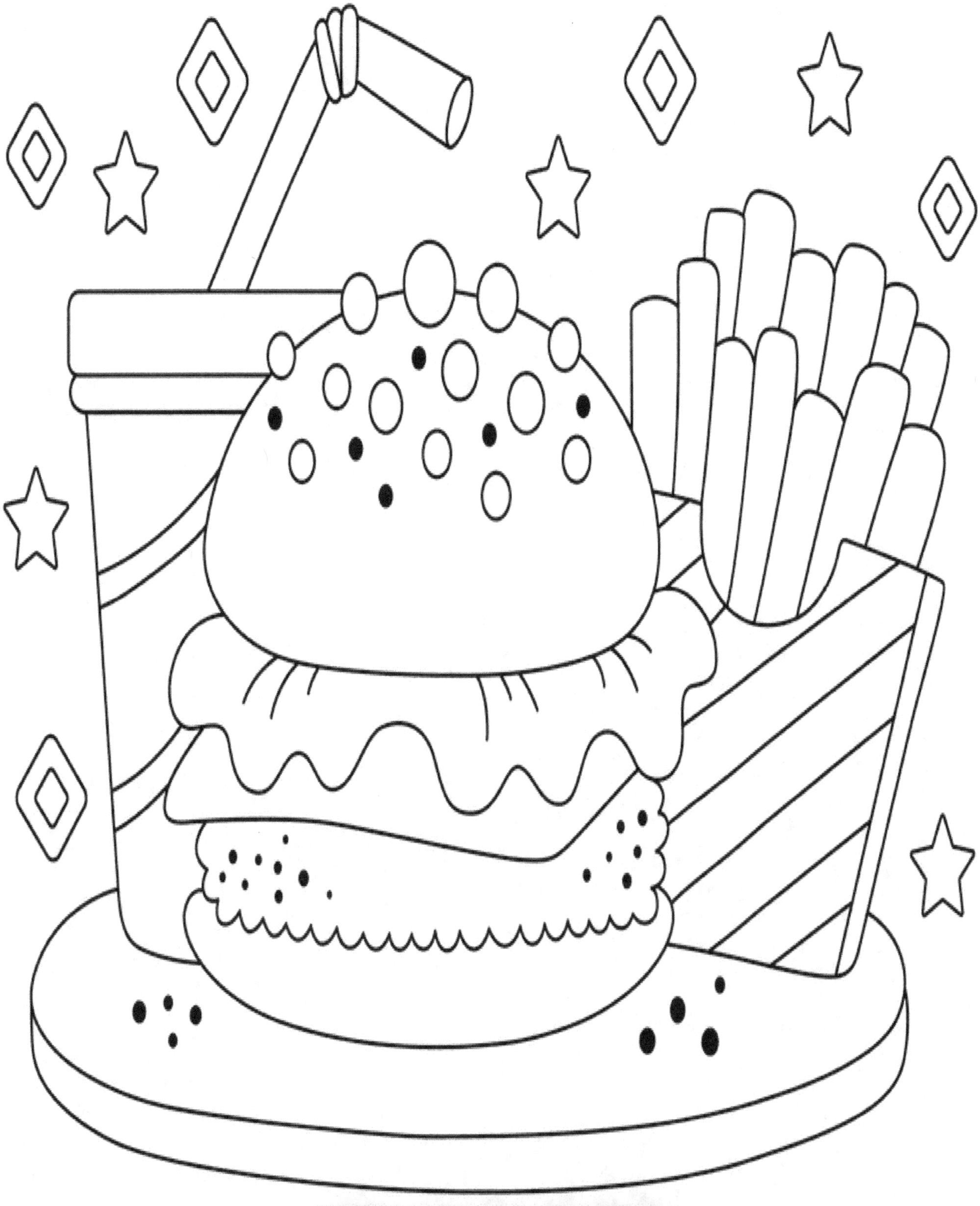

BURGER

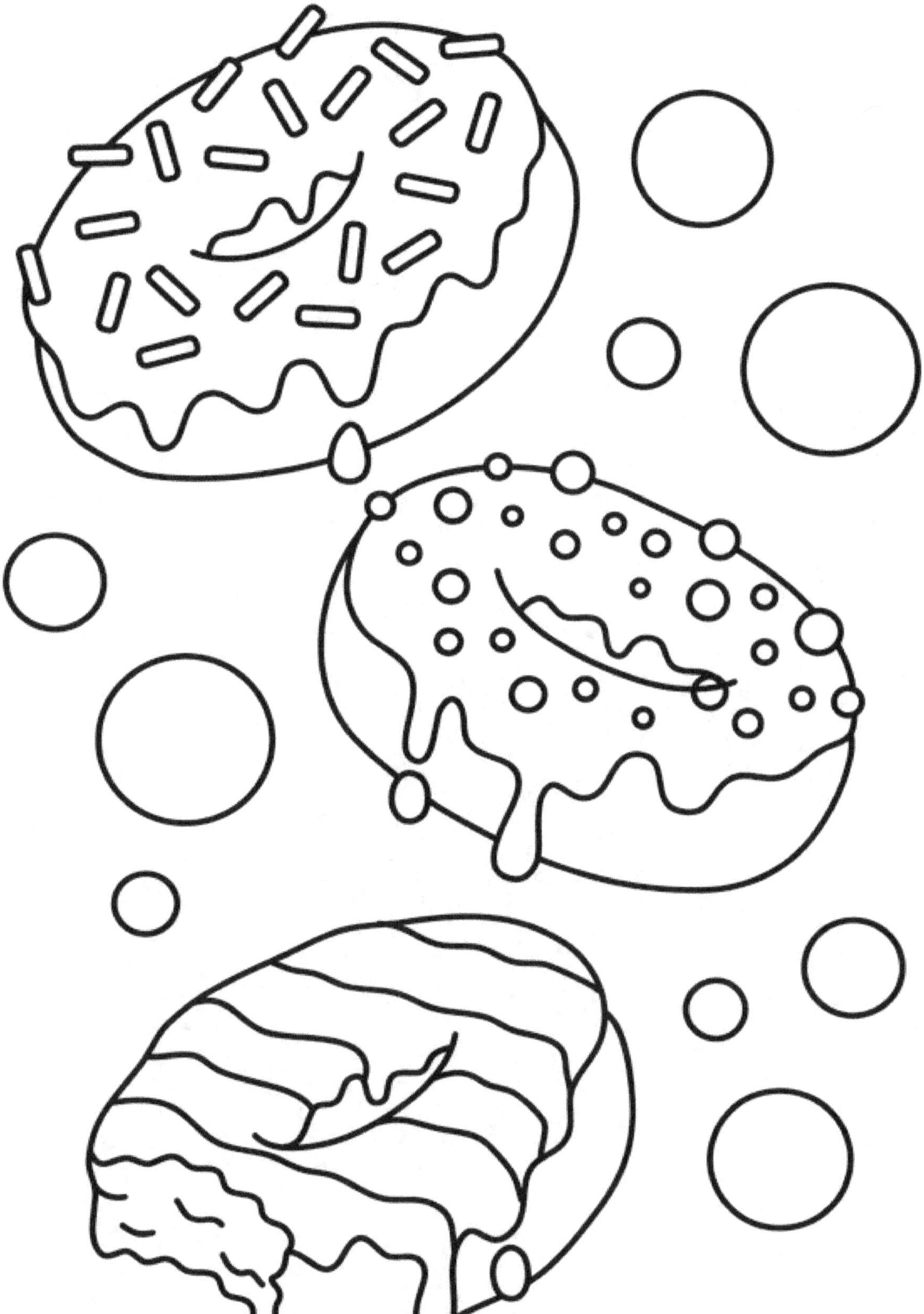

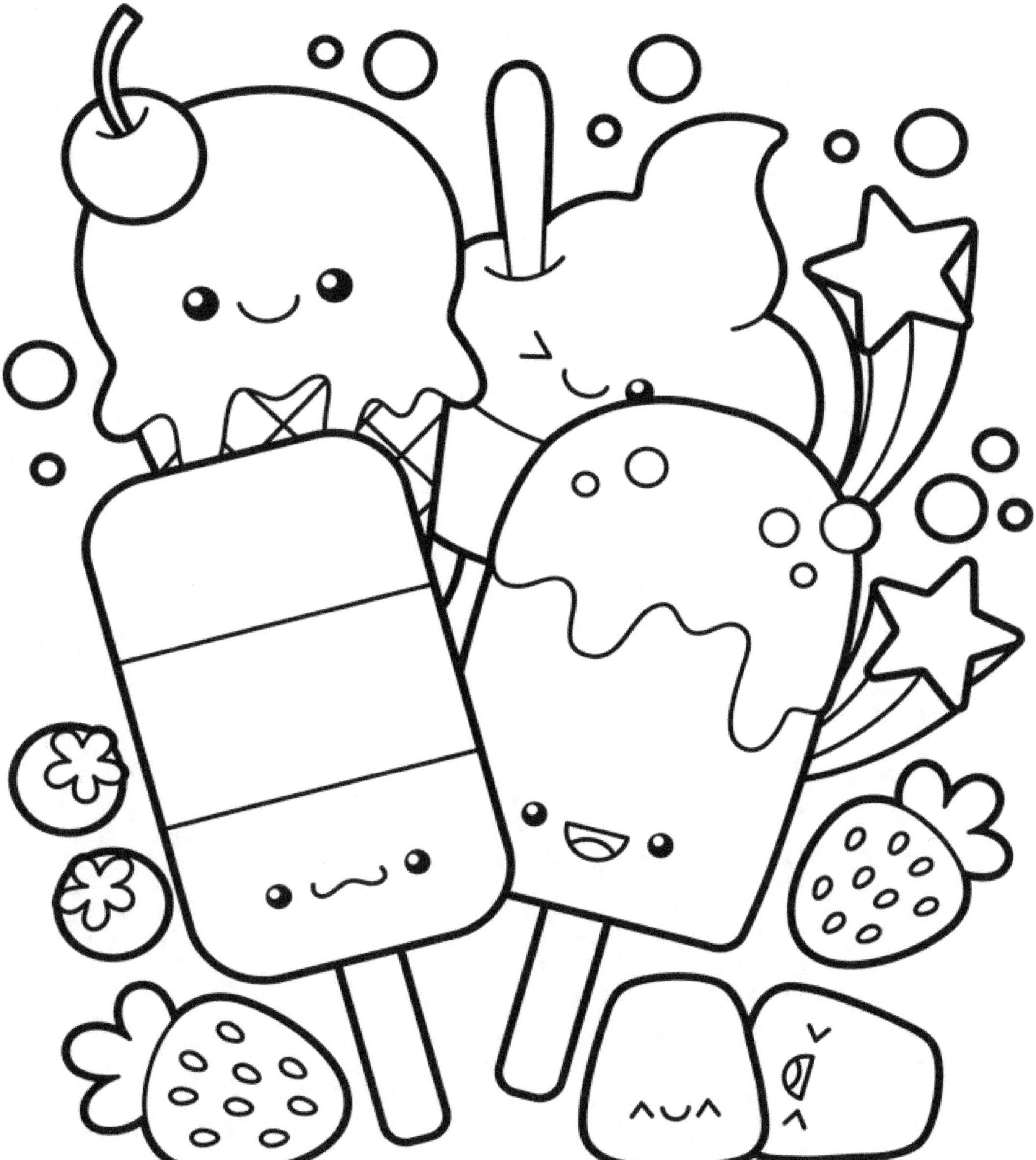

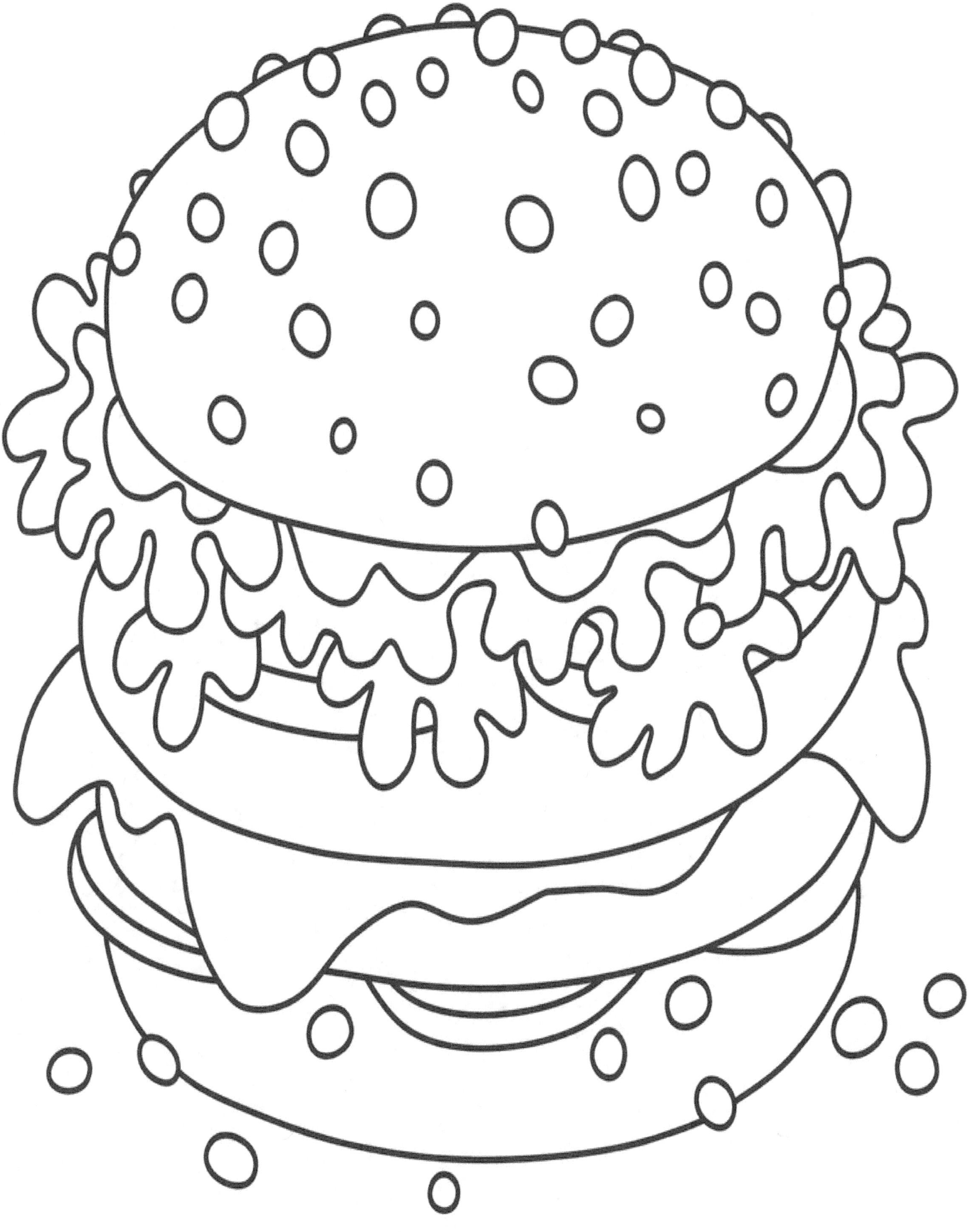

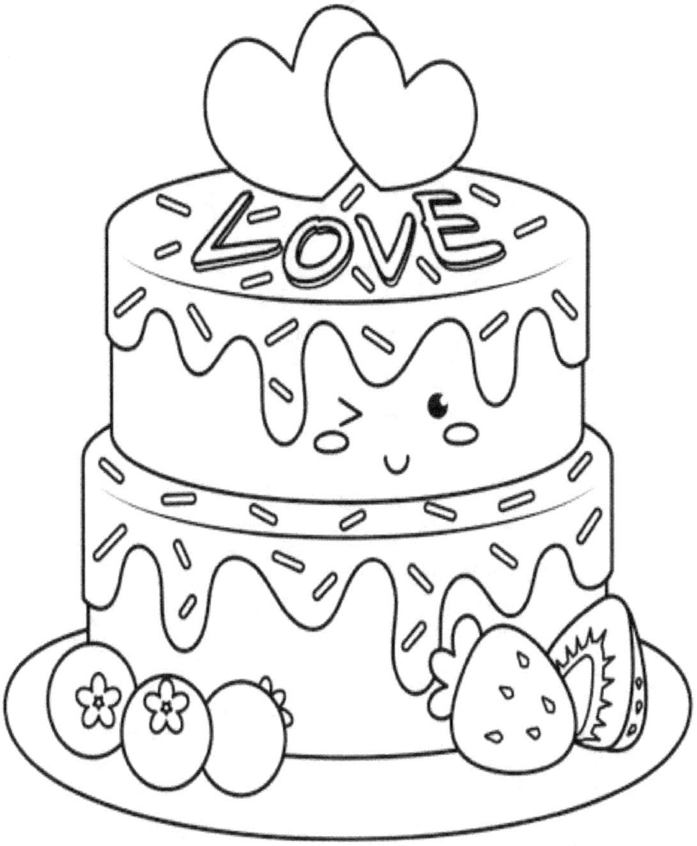
LOVE
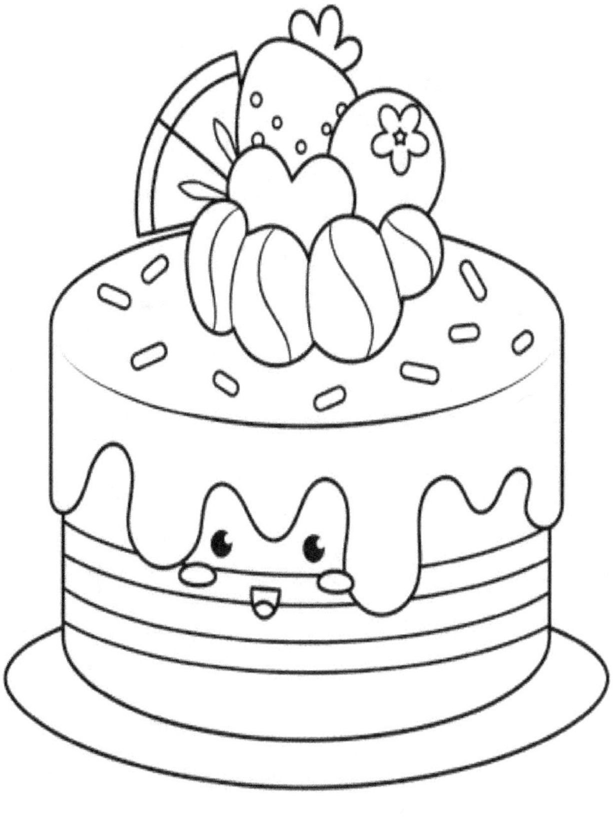
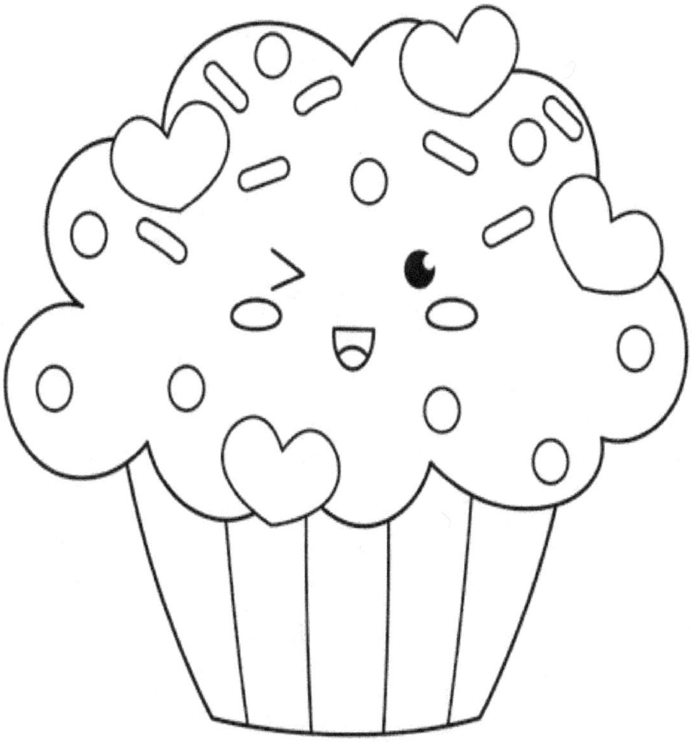
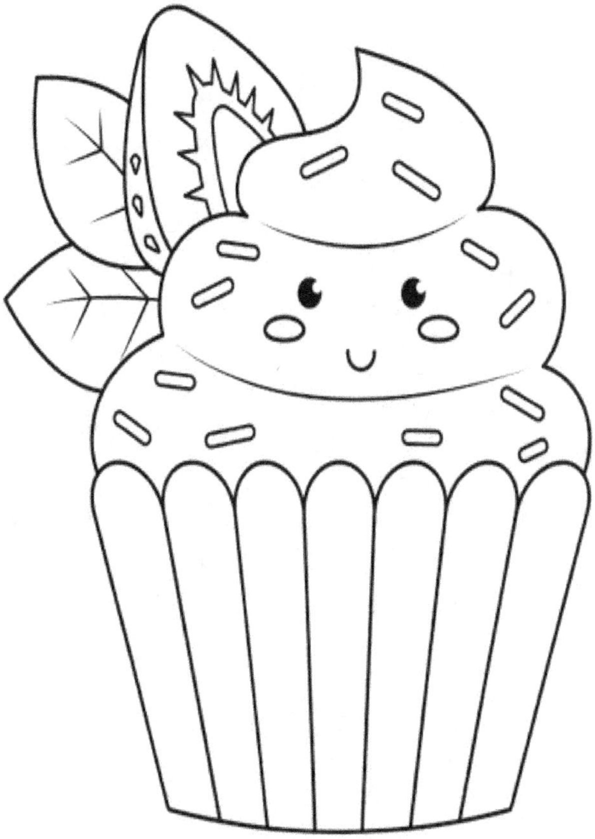

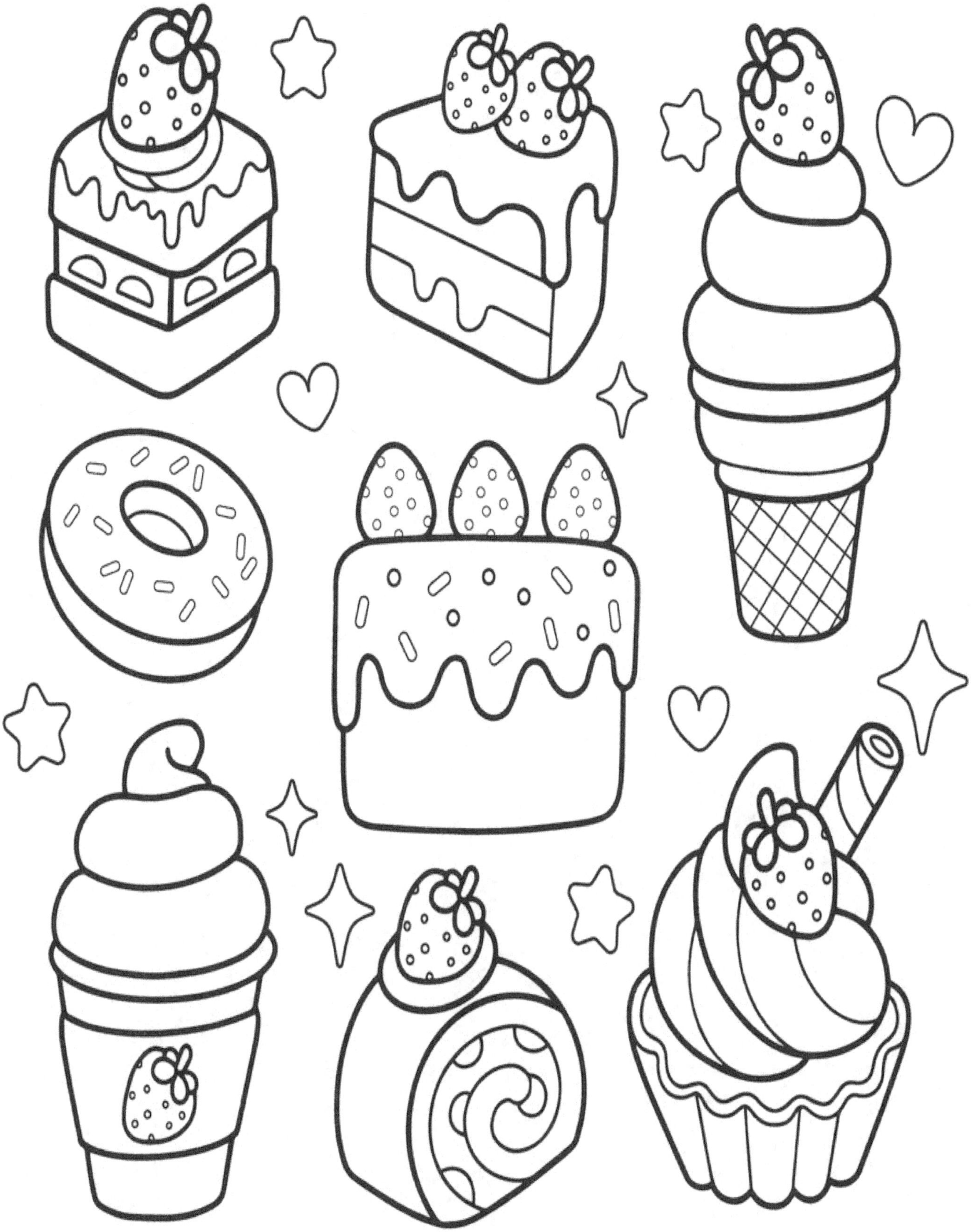

www.ingramcontent.com/pod-product-compliance
Lightning Source LLC
Chambersburg PA
CBHW082215220526
45470CB00010B/3180
* 9 7 9 8 3 2 4 4 0 6 1 7 2 *